THE THEORY
AND PRACTICE
OF MEDITATION

THE THEORY AND PRACTICE OF MEDITATION

Second Edition, Revised
and Expanded

Edited by
Rudolph M. Ballentine, M.D.

Published by

THE HIMALAYAN INTERNATIONAL
INSTITUTE OF YOGA SCIENCE AND
PHILOSOPHY OF THE USA
Honesdale, Pennsylvania

©1986 by The Himalayan International Institute
of Yoga Science and Philosophy of the U.S.A.
RR 1, Box 400
Honesdale, Pennsylvania 18431

The paper used in this publication meets the minimum requirements of
American National Standard for Information Sciences—Permanence
of Paper for Printed Library Materials, ANSI Z39.48–1984. ∞

Library of Congress Cataloging in Publication Data:

The Theory and practice of meditation.

　　　Rev. ed. of: The theory & practice of meditation.
c1975.
　　　1. Meditation.　I. Ballentine, Rudolph, 1941–
II. Theory & practice of meditation.
BL627.T49　1986　　158'.12　　86-9802
ISBN 0-89389-075-8

Contents

Introduction 1

What Is Meditation? 9
Swami Rama

Obstacles in Meditation 35
Rudolph M. Ballentine, M.D.

Meditation in Action 49
Swami Ajaya, Ph.D.

Mind, Meditation, and Emotions 67
Phil Nuernberger, Ph.D.

Meditation and Meaning in Life 93
Arpita, Ph.D.

Meditation and the Unconscious Mind 109
Rudolph M. Ballentine, M.D.

The Tradition of Superconscious Meditation 135
Pandit Usharbudh Arya, D.Litt.

Appendix A: Breathing Exercises 151

Appendix B: Beginning the Practice of
Meditation 159

About the Authors 163

Introduction

This book is a collection of articles by some of the best-versed scholars and professional persons writing on yoga, Eastern thought, and meditation in the West today. The contributors to this volume are unique not only for their knowledge but also for their sincere and thoroughgoing efforts to integrate the principles they have learned and taught into their own lives and work. This gives their writings a freshness and simplicity that can come only from those who base their words on firsthand experience.

Those who have accomplished to some degree an incorporation of the life of meditation into the fabric of their thought and work may find themselves overwhelmed by the simple question, "What is meditation?" How to describe something that is so simple in essence and yet so complex in its ramifications? Together, the essays in this volume provide a well-rounded examination and explication of both the nature and the process of meditation. This book is designed to provide the reader with a solid grounding in this vital art and science. This new edition of *The Theory and Practice of Meditation* has been extensively revised and expanded. We hope it will be useful both to the beginning student and also to those experienced students who want a deeper understanding of the practice of meditation.

The first article, "What Is Meditation?," is written by

Swami Rama. Though he has not attempted to establish a popular following either in his homeland or in the West, among the teachers of yoga and meditation in India he is regarded with respect and reverence. University-educated and appointed to the high post of Shankaracharya at an unprecedentedly young age, he left this position to carry the tradition of meditation to other parts of the world. Though the depth and breadth of his knowledge is vast, Swami Rama here offers us a delightfully simple and yet surprisingly comprehensive description of both the aims and the means of meditation. As the first article makes clear, meditation is an easy-to-learn inward method that, if consistently practiced, leads to a knowledge of oneself on all levels. As Swami Rama points out, the essence of yoga is the discovery and exploration of the world within oneself. The various practices of yoga are designed to prepare for and to facilitate this inner voyage. The article also describes six steps that lead one to the awareness of the inner reality and discusses the role played in this process by the personal teacher.

The next chapter, "Obstacles in Meditation," explores the most common barriers or obstacles that individuals experience when they begin the practice of meditation. Experienced students may find it helpful in answering many questions about their experience. It indicates specific techniques to eliminate obstacles to one's progress, so that one can enjoy the deepening experience of meditation without frustration or unnecessary difficulty.

In "Meditation in Action," Swami Ajaya describes an approach to our daily lives that can make all our waking hours an extension of the meditative process. Far from being an escape from the world, meditation is a way of enhancing our ability to function in the world creatively, constructively, and peacefully. Swami Ajaya speaks from a unique vantage point as both a swami and a practicing clinical psychologist, and his chapter describes the ways we can use meditation to live independently and joyfully.

As Dr. Phil Nuernberger points out in his article, "Mind, Meditation, and Emotions," the mind and emotions are major determining factors in health and disease. Emotional balance and harmony are the result of understanding ourselves on all levels. Through meditation we develop our powers of internal concentration, and we become aware of our internal processes, leading to the ability to transform negative emotional states to the positive emotions of love, joy, and tranquility. As meditation deepens, we experience our true identity as one of calmness and nonattachment, and we are able to be creative in the world without identifying with the ups and downs of our personalities or our previous attachments, desires, and dependencies.

The next contributor, Dr. Arpita, writes on the usefulness of meditation in coming to terms with the basic issues of life. Trained in Western psychology, Dr. Arpita also has extensive experience in teaching the philosophy and psychology of the meditative tradition. Inner happiness, she reminds us, cannot be achieved without a sense of meaning and purpose in life. Meditation relieves the core stress of human life; it is the effective and conscious way to solve the essential problem of spiritual unrest and emptiness.

The next article, entitled "Meditation and the Unconscious Mind," explains how a systematic approach to meditation helps us to study the mind and to bring about a gradual expansion of consciousness and transformation of our personality. It examines the process by which our conscious mind is continuously functioning to maintain and reinforce our characteristic self-identity and explains how the practice of meditation can help us learn to identify with progressively higher and more expansive self-concepts. By becoming an uninvolved witness or a dispassionate observer to our habitual mental functioning, we allow our subconscious impressions to come into awareness and become integrated into our personality. The article then describes how meditation can help us create the conditions to reduce the ego's defensiveness so that the process of observation can be facilitated and we can become actively involved in a process of ever-increasing psychic integration and self-realization.

The concluding article in this collection is a description of the tradition of Superconscious Meditation. The author, Dr. Usharbudh Arya, is a renowned Sanskrit scholar and pandit. In this essay he outlines for us the concepts and tenets of this great tradition. He explains the nature of the Superconscious, and relates the basic themes of the principal texts on which this tradition is based. He explains to us the simple yet revolutionary idea that consciousness forms the seed (*bindu*) out of which the phenomenal world takes shape. This is both the essence of Eastern philosophy and the basis of Superconscious Meditation.

Finally, the Appendixes systematically describe several of the specific breathing exercises that are referred to in these articles. As these writings make clear, the breathing exercises presented here constitute an important preparatory and preliminary part of meditation. A clear, concise introduction to the technique of meditation is also included.

The essays collected in this book deliberately range from the philosophical and poetic to the pragmatic and down-to-earth. For the questioning beginner, meditation is defined, described, and examined in terms of its philosophy, psychology, and techniques of application. By approaching the basic definition of meditation from several important perspectives, the contributors to this volume have been able to offer the reader what is designed to be both the most comprehensive and the most practical introduction to the subject of meditation that is currently available.

Rudolph M. Ballentine, M.D.

What Is Meditation?
Swami Rama

The method of meditation is an inward process that leads one to the fountain of life and light. This is the center of consciousness, from where consciousness flows on various degrees and grades. A human being is a citizen of two worlds: the world within and the world without. To create a bridge between these two requires human effort, but it is possible for one to do so; it is possible to live in the world and yet remain above it.

This art of living and being has its source in the method of meditation. That which cannot be taught by modern education can be understood and realized by practicing meditation. No one teaches modern people how to be still and they never find the time and opportunity to be still. To be still is a must for meditation; for only then can the truth or the Reality within reveal itself.

So meditation is a method of knowing truth, that which is within every human being. Meditation is a simple technique that can be learned in a few minutes, but it is a very practical subject, and the benefits of meditation are immense.

There are many steps for attaining the highest state of meditation, and anyone who desires to practice can attain a state of meditation within a few months. The first benefit of meditation is freedom from stress and strain; the second benefit is clarity of mind; and the third benefit is knowledge of one's own internal states. Then one is established in one's essential nature, which is happiness, peace, and bliss. Meditation helps one to attain the highest level of equilibrium and tranquility. With persistence, it leads one to the state of *turiya*, the state beyond.

But to attain these benefits, one must understand that knowledge is within, and that one will have to practice. Practice will make one perfect. Without practice, one cannot have inner experience, and without this experience one cannot be guided. Experience should be one's guide. Meditation shows one how to know within oneself. There is no mystery in this method. It is a practical and systematic technique that leads one to peace and knowledge. If one knows all the things of the world and does not realize one's inner potential, how can one enjoy life, and how can one attain the purpose of life?

The greatest of all enjoyments is the tranquil state that can be attained through meditation. Often students get excited and want to attain the highest state in a few days' time, forgetting that this inward method of learning through meditation is not like other learning programs. It is an unlearning program, a journey without movement— one advances without any external movement. One remains still and yet attains one's goal.

Meditation Is Not Religion

Meditation teaches one how to be; it is an inward method for knowing oneself on all levels and for experiencing the higher levels of consciousness. The basic instruction for meditation is, "Be still, and know that I am God," and this is also the very core of the Bible.

But meditation does not interfere with any religious or cultural beliefs. Meditation should not be mingled with any sort of religion, and religious ceremony should not be involved in meditation. Doing so could create needless conflict with one's cultural and religious background and personal beliefs. If a teacher involves any religious ceremony in meditation, it would be better not to learn from that person.

The word "meditation" has been used by various religions, but not with its proper meaning: real meditation is entirely different from the sense in which the word is used by religionists. The different religious groups of the world give people a code for what to do and what not to do, but the question of how to *be* remains unanswered.

In the English dictionary the word "meditation" has not been adequately explained as yet. It is defined as meaning to ruminate on, to reflect upon, or to contemplate—that's all. But in the Sanskrit, Tibetan, Chinese, and Japanese languages, the word "meditation" has been used in a very clear way: it means to make the mind free from disturbing thoughts. Meditation is a method that makes one aware of Reality. This is an inward journey from the gross, to the subtle, to the most subtle aspect of one's being.

The purpose of the tradition of meditation is to lead one to the center of consciousness, from where consciousness flows on various degrees and grades. The purpose of meditation is not to convert one from Christianity to Judaism, for example, or from Hinduism to Zen. Meditation neither rejects nor recognizes any particular religion.

Meditation is an inward method that leads one to the center of consciousness by stilling the mind. There is no other way of education that helps one to know oneself on all levels. There is no religion that does this, either—and if there is any philosophy that speaks of this, it is not helpful, because it is purely theoretical without any practice.

The practical aspect of religion is missing from daily life, no matter which religious tradition one comes from. "Knowing thyself" is the aim of everyone's life, and for that, one must practice an inward method. The ancients of all great religions of the world knew the method of meditation, but modern humanity is lost in the charms and attractions of materialism. This is a self-created misery.

What Meditation Isn't

Just as many people think meditation is part of religion, they also confuse the words "meditation" and "contemplation." If one looks up the word "meditation" in the dictionary, he will find it defined as "contemplation," and "contemplation" is defined as "meditation," as if there were no difference between the two, but they are actually two different things.

Contemplation is thinking with a definite idea in mind, but in meditation one does not explore the various aspects of a particular concept. In meditation one has a single point of focus, and one does not change that—it is always the same focus. For contemplation one needs an idea, but to learn meditation one needs an object of concentration.

Meditation will tell one how distracted one's mind is, how much concentration one has. But meditation itself is different from concentration. To concentrate is to narrow down, to lead the mind one-pointedly in one direction. Meditation is expansion, but if the mind is scattered and dissipated, there is nothing to expand. Without concentration, meditation is not possible.

Some schools of meditation want to please people, and so they say that one does not have to do anything particular to practice meditation. But they are misleading and hurting people, because it is not possible to direct the the mind inward one-pointedly without concentration.

Meditation is a self-reliant method of inner study, and it therefore should not be confused with anything like hypnosis. Hypnosis can definitely help one in dealing with many dissipated and distorted conditions of the mind, and a therapist should use all the available resources to help patients, but it does not make one independent, however, and so it cannot be included in a self-training program. Modern education is totally based on hypnosis, or suggestion. Education based on suggestion or autosuggestion is superficial and is not truthful.

What is the difference between hypnosis and meditation? Many of the books written on this topic are by people who have not experienced both systems, and so they cannot understand the differences between them. Hypnosis imposes control on the mind, and then one is not oneself, but meditation is going within, beneath all these different forms and names.

The purpose of meditation is to lead one to unity, to a realization that we are all breathing the same air and that there is only one proprietor who is giving the same vitality to you and me. In meditation, one learns the process that makes one aware of the unity of life within all these multiples. Meditation makes a person aware of oneness, whereas hypnosis makes a person aware of manyness. One unites; the other divides. One is internal; the other is external.

Meditation leads one to the silence within. Most people don't know what silence is. They have never enjoyed it. They may go to a quiet room where there is no outer sound, but the mind remains noisy all the time. How can external silence lead one to internal silence? The mind will start becoming more active when one is silent externally. But when one learns to love the silence within, then the highest of all joys becomes that deep silence in which one goes beyond all the states of one's mind. The mind then turns within and enjoys that peace beyond.

Preparation for Meditation

Before one is ready for meditation, there are two necessary steps one has to practice. First one should learn to train one's attention, and then one should learn to concentrate; only then can one learn meditation. One should learn to pay attention toward what one does.

Typically, our minds are restless and confused; our attention flits from one thought to another. Through the course of a single day we may experience many unpleasant emotions, such as anxiety, depression, disappointment, anger, and frustration. We are pulled here and there by the many desires we have. We are easily distracted and have difficulty finding a center of equilibrium. There is scarcely a chance to find rest and renewal. But meditation is a practice that from the very beginning helps us find stability and calmness. We become freed from our restless desires, from the disturbing thoughts that normally come into our minds, and from our emotional reactions. As we progress in the practice of meditation, we come to find that these disturbances are gradually replaced by an ever-increasing sense of peace and happiness. Our mental and emotional environment becomes uplifted, and we experience a sense of inner refreshment and joy.

Through meditation an aspirant's cognition, emotion, and volition become unified, and his latent powers are awakened. Only through such a total integration of the mind can one develop a dynamic personality. All the glorious deeds in human history have been achieved by people of concentrated willpower. Western psychologists, psychiatrists, and physiologists have begun to realize that the human mind can be resolved through meditation. Meditation begins with concentration. Through concentration the mind becomes steady and one-pointed. When concentration leads to the uninterrupted flow of the mind toward one object, this becomes meditation. The mind is then expanded to the higher realms of the superconscious state. Thus, meditation is the process through which the mind is first made one-pointed and then expanded to the state of enlightenment. It involves a subtle yet definite effort, which then leads man to the superconscious state.

Once the mind becomes one pointed, it is a tremendous force. It can create miracles in the world and can increase the happiness and well-being of others. A one-pointed mind bestows immense physical, neural, mental, and spiritual benefits.

The States of Consciousness

The school of meditation talks about the body, mind, and spirit in the following way: one has a body, but he is not the body. Next, when one starts observing himself, one comes to know that he is a breathing being also, and then finally he learns that he is a thinking being too. When one examines his thinking process, one finds that during a certain period he thinks, and at other times he starts dreaming, or goes into a deeper state of unconsciousness called sleep. Thus, one experiences three states of mind: waking, dreaming, and sleeping.

The conscious part of the mind is trained by our educational system, but there is no systematic education anywhere that trains the unconscious mind, the totality of the mind. So far, most people have been trained and educated to see, watch, and verify things externally, but they do not know how to understand their own internal states.

No one teaches people how to dream or how to sleep or what happens to the mind when one dreams and sleeps, so only a small part of the mind is being educated by the so-called educational system. No one teaches that one can go beyond the three states of waking, dreaming, and sleeping. We do not learn how we would feel or what our known experience would be beyond these three known states of mind. If one is not able to go beyond these three states of mind, then one cannot establish a link between the unconscious and the center of consciousness.

Meditation is the method that teaches us how to know all these states. So, if one really wants to understand oneself, one should invest some time in meditation. But if one does not know the correct method of meditation, one should not sit in a pose of meditation and thus waste one's time and energy. If, however, one merely learns to sit quietly, to breathe deeply, and to gently allow all one's thoughts to go away, then even this first step will be very helpful and relaxing. Deeper states and higher steps of meditation will lead one to self-realization, to a higher level of being.

There are two methods for beginning the practice of meditation. One method is to know first and then to tread the path; the other method is to start practicing, and through experience to then know the truth.

The first path says one should gather enough information through books, teachers, seminars, sages, and sayings, and then, with doubts dispelled, follow the path that millions have followed before. The other approach says one should start practicing and let his experience guide him. Both of these paths should be united—one should learn and know, and at the same time practice.

No one is fully happy when treading the path of the external world. Yet the path of meditation does not condemn the external path. The external path is full of means, but it is not the end. If one is searching for the end, for fulfillment, by following the external path, then he is searching in the wrong place.

The method of meditation systematically leads one to the source of consciousness through experiencing various levels, one after another. Whenever the mind goes from one experiential state to another, it is a new experience, and the mind will definitely be bewildered and confused. One is already confused, though, so one should not be afraid of this temporary new confusion or want to give up. One should learn to understand all the other levels of consciousness.

This path does not promise that one will meet God. People have been wanting this for ages, creating misery for themselves, and having little solace. But they are not understanding Reality. The path of meditation will not give one anything that one does not already have. The path of meditation will lead one to oneself on all levels.

People know themselves only on one level, and therefore they think they are small and limited: they are confused and hate themselves. But the path of meditation says this petty self is not the true Self. When one knows the Reality, one knows that there is no difference between the Reality and oneself. One realizes, "I am That." This is the purpose of the path of meditation.

History of the Meditative Science

The science of meditation was developed systematically in ancient India during the Upanishadic period and was later elaborated by the seer Patanjali. The meditative practices that were developed spread far and wide. A school of meditation was established by Indian monks in Egypt around the third century B.C. and in China by the fourth century A.D. Later the teachings were carried to Japan; in fact the word *Zen* is derived from the Sanskrit word *dhyana,* which means meditation. In the Christian tradition a school of meditation was established by St. Anthony, and the methods of meditation were known to saints such as St. Francis and others. However, because of fear that it would become the object of religious persecution, the art of meditation remained secretly hidden in the sacred bosom of a few wise saints.

Over the centuries meditation has developed into a highly evolved and systematic science for expanding consciousness. In yoga blind faith is always discouraged. Instead, certain methods and the results that can be achieved through their use are described, and the aspirant is expected to convince himself or herself of their validity only by trying them and achieving the results mentioned. In this empirical approach a person's firsthand experience of a state of consciousness is his only meaningful proof of its existence. No other proof can be given, nor is any other proof necessary. In his *Yoga Sutras,* Patanjali mentions certain powers a yogi may acquire through concentration and meditation. For example, through sustained and prolonged concentration on the hollow of the throat, a yogi can transcend hunger and thirst. Such a claim is verified only by practicing the concentration specified.

Yoga is a voyage of self-discovery. The student explores his inner self aided by the directions of the illumined yogis who have trodden the same paths and reached the final goal. Such directions, both general and specific, are given by Patanjali in his *Yoga Sutras* and in other manuals. However, in treading a specific path, each of us must seek the aid of a guru, a spiritual teacher and guide. The word guru means "darkness dispeller," and thus the guru is the one who has the power to help us dispel the darkness of ignorance. In the West, however, this word has become misused, and people may say "I am a guru" without having themselves attained such goals.

Methods of Meditation

Let us now consider the methods of meditation. Before the aspirant can attain a state of meditation he should practice six preliminary steps. Every time one meditates, he or she should go through these six pre-liminary stages, if he is to reach a meditative state.

1. The first step is to establish the right mental atmosphere. Being mindful of the *yamas* and *niyamas,* the ten principles of living graciously in the world and expanding one's self-awareness, helps the student to compose his mind and establish harmony within.

The five *yamas* (restraints) and five *niyamas* (observances) together constitute the "ten commitments" of yoga. The *yamas* are *ahimsa*, nonviolence; *satya*, truthfulness; *asteya*, nontheft; *brahmacharya*, nonsensuality; and *aparigraha*, nonpossessiveness. The *niyamas* are *saucha*, purity; *santosha*, contentment; *tapas*, asceticism; *svadhyaya*, self-study; and *Ishvara-pranidhana*, surrender of the ego to the higher Self.

For instance, if one is in an angry mood, he should try to wash away his anger by reminding himself of the principle of *ahimsa*, or non-harming. Paying mental homage to the guru and to the long line of sages through whom he has received the teaching also helps the student in establishing a favorable mental atmosphere.

2. Before the student assumes the meditative posture it is helpful to go through some relaxation exercises. These exercises are practiced in the corpse posture (*shavasana*). Relaxation can be achieved on three levels: relaxation of the physical body (the muscles and joints); relaxation of the nervous system and internal organs; and relaxation of the mind. The exercises range from the elementary ones to very advanced ones that aim at withdrawing into the subtle body. Relaxation with deep breathing proceeds systematically from head to toe and back upward. A systematic description of this exercise is given in Appendix A.

Relaxation and concentration are intertwined. One cannot concentrate when one is tense, for tension implies restlessness and disturbance both in the physical body and in the mind. Systematic relaxation leads the mind toward concentration as it focuses in turn on the various parts of the body. Each muscle and joint is relaxed completely through such concentration. Relaxation exercises have been used to cure hypertension, migraine headaches, and the like. The physical relaxation leads to calmness of the mind. Alpha brain waves predominate in the relaxed state. In the more advanced relaxation exercises, theta waves (which are indicative of concentration and creativity) predominate.

3. Having relaxed the body, nerves, and mind, the aspirant assumes a meditative posture that is steady and comfortable and ensures that head, neck, and trunk are erect and in a straight line. The body should be made relaxed and absolutely motionless, thus bringing under control the *karmendriyas,* or active senses. The aspirant will find that, as time goes by, merely sitting motionless in a meditative posture will induce a feeling of peace and joy.

4. Sitting in the meditative posture, the aspirant next practices some breathing exercises (*pranayama*) which involve control of the breath and vital energy, and bring about purification of the body and nervous system. The exercises discussed below are discussed in detail in Appendix A. The *kapalabhati* and *bhastrika* exercises empty the stale air from the lungs, increase the oxygen supply to the body, and make the mind more alert and free from drowsiness. The sinus and respiratory passages also clear up with time. Breathing becomes deeper and more even. The *nadi shodhana pranayama* (channel purification) strengthens the nervous system, purifies the energy channels, or *nadis,* and clears the mind. The right and left breath are equalized, and the breath becomes deeper and more gentle. These breathing exercises lead the aspirant to the deeper stages of sense withdrawal and concentration.

5. The fifth step is *pratyahara,* the control and balance of the *jnanendriyas,* or the senses of perception. The

aspirant mentally withdraws from thinking about other places and becomes aware of the space immediately around him. He withdraws his awareness from all other times, and experiences the present moment more completely. He tries to be "here and now." He then makes a determination, or a *sankalpa*, by mentally affirming, "I am not the body, I am not the senses—they are my instruments. I am not the mind—the mind is my subtler instrument. I am the *Atman*, the Infinite." Every time the mind tries to wander outward, the aspirant gently draws it back inward.

6. The aspirant then tries to make his mind one-pointed through voluntary attention and concentration. He becomes aware of his breath and synchronizes it with a mantra such as *soham*, "I am That." "Sooooo . . ." is synchronized with the in-breath and "Hummmm . . ." with the out-breath. The aspirant begins by concentrating on the breath in the nostrils. This concentration makes the mind one-pointed, but prolonged concentration enables one to go further, piercing the conscious and subconscious and expanding the mind to the level of the superconscious. Not all methods of concentration will lead to the superconscious; only methods prescribed by the guru based on his evaluation of the aspirant's capacity and needs will lead to the superconscious state. One needs the guidance and grace of the guru.

Guru and Mantra

The first stage in guidance is initiation into a specific *mantra*. Then the aspirant may be given a concentration on a particular sound, light, or *chakra,* along with the mantra. Through successful concentration on a chakra, or center of integration, the spiritual energy of that center is awakened and the blocked channels of subtle energy (*nadis*) are opened. This cannot be accomplished by the aspirant on his own, but is possible only through the initiatory power of a guru. The guru is a channel for power flowing down the long line of gurus dating back many thousands of years. There are more advanced stages of initiation beyond this, one following another, until the aspirant reaches full realization of his divine nature through the grace of the guru.

In meditation a conscious, voluntary attempt is made to still the activity of the conscious mind. Through withdrawal of the senses and concentration, one-pointedness of mind is achieved. Then, like the continuous flow of oil from one vessel to another, concentration flows into meditation. The uninterrupted flow of the mind leads to timelessness, and intuitive knowledge dawns. The transition from the one-pointedness of the conscious mind to expansion into the superconscious is possible only through the grace of the guru. Without such grace the aspirant may, through concentration, still the conscious mind and then become aware only of the murky depths of the subconscious. The subconscious is a maze of diverse impressions. The aspirant, without a teacher's guidance, may lose himself in this maze and be unable to transcend the subconscious to attain the superconscious state. The occult sciences and black magic are based on the experience of the dark shadows of the subconscious. This state represents a fall from the conscious to the subconscious rather than an ascent from the conscious into the purity of the superconscious.

Let us consider some of the concentrations that, when prescribed by a guru, lead to the superconscious experience. These concentrations may be mentioned in detail in books, but they do not take the aspirant very far unless they are personally prescribed for one's use by the guru.

In the fourth chapter of Patanjali's *Yoga Sutras,* various methods of meditation are outlined according to the capacity and ability of the aspirant. One such method is mantra yoga. A mantra is a secret teaching imparted by the guru to his disciple when the disciple is initiated into the yoga tradition. The word *mantra* means "that which liberates the mind from all griefs, sorrows, and agonies." A mantra consists of one or more words chosen by the guru specifically for leading a particular aspirant to the final truth; not every word is a mantra. Mantras are not composed by a guru; mantras have been handed down through the meditative tradition, having been revealed to great yogis and seers while they were in a superconscious state. The science of mantra is very exact, but very few people know or understand its significance. Once initiated, the disciple repeats and meditates upon his mantra throughout his life, and gradually the mantra leads him to the stage of *samadhi.*

Japa is the act of repeating the mantra. Japa has to become an essential part of the aspirant's life. Starting with mere repetition of the mantra, the disciple is led spontaneously to meditate upon its meaning and then to the realization of the truth it contains. The mantra also works on the level of his subconscious mind, controlling his moods and combating and overcoming undesirable emotional states, such as anger, greed, lust, sloth, and the like. It purifies his mind, making him capable of the degree of concentration necessary for his subsequent evolution into superconsciousness. The practice of japa is found in most religions of the world and is considered a form of prayer by those who employ it.

In the scriptures it is said that when the disciple is ready, the guru appears. The guru need not be a human being. In the yogic scriptures there are many instances of aspirants having been initiated in their dreams by great saints. The mantra received in such a dream experience is considered to be as sacred as those received in the waking state from a human guru. Of course, the aspirant should be careful not to believe that all of his dreams are of divine origin. The truly inspired dream experience brings with it a sense of joyous revelation and is easily distinguished from other dreams. Meditation upon such a dream experience is also one of the alternative methods of meditation.

The Self

The ultimate goal of meditation is to experience the Self or Atman. The Self is pure consciousness. The experience of Self is a state of transcendent knowledge and bliss; it is that state beyond time, space, and causation, which has been called *samadhi, nirvana,* cosmic consciousness, and many other names. When the mind is completely centered for an extended period of time, when it is not distracted by various thoughts or external objects, it becomes aware of the essence of our being, the Atman. Ordinarily, awareness is not refined enough to perceive the Self because the mind is preoccupied with more gross perceptions and thoughts. The practice of meditation gradually sharpens our perception of the inner working of the real Self that is hidden within.

The Atman is covered by three sheaths. The outermost is the physical sheath composed of gross matter. Beneath this is the subtle sheath composed of subtler counterparts of gross matter. The innermost sheath is the causal sheath, which has been fashioned out of our actions according to the law of karma. In normal waking consciousness all three sheaths intervene between the aspirant and Atman. During the dream state the physical sheath is removed. In the state of dreamless sleep, only the causal sheath shrouds Atman. This final sheath is difficult to penetrate, which is why one cannot achieve the realization of Atman merely through dreamless sleep. In the state of dreamless sleep we are closest to Atman, but no memory of this experience remains when we wake up. One method of meditation consists of trying to bring back into the waking state the experience of the state of dreamless sleep. This method involves dwelling upon and trying to strengthen the sense of peace that lingers into the waking state after experiencing the dreamless sleep.

In the Upanishads it is stated that the Atman dwells within the lotus of the heart. Here, the words "lotus of the heart" do not refer to the heart of flesh but to the *anahata chakra*. In the *Katha Upanishad* the Atman is described as a smokeless, pure, illumined flame the size of the thumb burning in the shrine of the heart. In their deeper states of meditation, yogis experience the lotus of the heart. Bathed in its inner light, they experience divine bliss. One of the more advanced methods of meditation consists of meditation upon the lotus of the heart after one has made one's mind steady through concentration. Withdrawing from the objects of the senses, one enters this shrine of Atman and, meditating on it, transcends the body and experiences higher knowledge.

When a student first begins to concentrate, he or she is faced with all sorts of distractions. Many aspirants grow discouraged, feeling that they were calmer before they started the practice. However, this feeling is only a result of experiencing disturbances that have always existed, but of which one was not previously aware. It is like seeing for the first time all the dust that has been swept under the carpet. This is only a stage or a transition, and if the aspirant perseveres, he or she will go beyond it and achieve the necessary one-pointedness of mind.

In the practice of concentration, the aspirant concerns himself or herself with the external aspects of objects. Concentration eventually gives way to meditation, in which one perceives the innermost nature of the object of concentration. Meditation leads to samadhi, in which the aspirant achieves oneness with the object of concentration.

In the lower stages of samadhi, though perfect concentration has been achieved, the seeds of desire and attachment still remain in a latent state. Liberation from all bondage comes only in the higher stages of samadhi when these seeds no longer exist. Then the mind is opened up to receive direct superconscious knowledge, which is beyond all perception of the senses and all comprehension of the intellect.

There are three processes that take place in the mind during meditation: contemplation, filling, and identification.

The aspirant should remember these three word-images before starting his meditation. Contemplate Atman, fill the mind with Atman, and then you will become identified with Atman. As you think, so you become; think you are Atman, and Atman you will become.

Meditation Through Self-Surrender

There is one method of yoga in which neither particular postures nor techniques of concentration or meditation are involved. This method—self-surrender—is the highest of all yogas and is described by Lord Krishna in the eighteenth chapter of the *Bhagavad Gita.* According to this method, one should surrender the body, mind, intellect, and ego entirely to the divine. The purpose of this method is to bring down into one's life the peace, purity, truth, consciousness, and bliss of the Supreme Self.

The qualities of peace and purity are often misunderstood. When we talk of peace, it is not the peace of the tomb to which we refer; rather it is a peace which permeates all aspects of life. This peace fuses our mind, actions, and speech, keeping us balanced and harmonized in all aspects of life. This peace illuminates our life. Its source is not found in temples, churches, or mosques, nor is it found in the rigidity of rituals and ceremonies or in the external worship of idols. It resides in the human soul as a manifestation of divine love. Purity means to accept no influence other than the influence of the divine. Mere external washing is meant to keep the body pure, but mental purity leads one from intellect to intuition.

Two other qualities of action characterize the life of the aspirant whose method is self-surrender: faithfulness and sincerity. Faithfulness is to admit and to manifest no movement other than that which is prompted and guided by the innermost consciousness. Sincerity requires the lifting of all the movements of mind, body, and action to the level of the highest consciousness and realization, where there is no individuality, duality, or body consciousness. Sincerity is the unification and harmonization of man around that one central will or divinity through which we speak, hear, think, and feel.

The Atman is revealed to that fortunate aspirant who surrenders himself without reserve to the Divine alone. For him, calmness, wisdom, and the seas of *ananda,* or bliss, overflow continuously. Merely wishing for self-surrender will not help. Merely assuming a mental attitude or having a number of inner experiences are not indications of self-surrender. Complete self-surrender requires a radical and total change in our lives. In this transformation all of our habits and actions should be surrendered and exposed to the divine light. Without self-surrender, divine wisdom is not possible. The unenlightened individual lives in the world as an animal, expressing only his own mind, action, and speech and satisfying only his own wants and desires. Establishing oneself in divinity and then bringing forward that divinity from the innermost level and expressing it through mind, action, and speech is a sacred process that does not require any effort other than self-surrender.

Without complete self-surrender it is quite impossible for the aspirant to get anywhere near his goal. In the course of this process he has to keep himself open to the call of the divine force and should allow that force to work through his thoughts, feelings, and actions. If one does not surrender, he is not allowing this force to work through him; he is imposing conditions upon it. Divine grace and bliss is ever-present, but we remain sleeping and unprepared to receive it in our daily life. This is the root cause of our bondage and misery.

In the early stages of practicing self-surrender, sincere effort is indispensable, but surrender is not a thing that can be done in a fit of emotion or in a day. The human ego resists surrender; the mind has its own ideas and clings to them. The ego holds sway over the unenlightened individual. We live in a world that is ruled by ego; unless a person sincerely desires to go beyond the mire of ego, self-surrender is impossible for him. If there is any surrender in the early stages of practice, it is of a doubtful nature, with selfish demands on it. But when spiritual powers awaken, true surrender occurs. A few aspirants begin with a true and dynamic will to surrender; they constantly dwell in the Self. Having once accepted self-surrender, they will not question it; thus they do not obstruct their own path.

Surrender is the way of accepting the divine. Surrender means to offer all one has and not to insist on the primacy of one's own ideas and desires. Surrender empties the aspirant of ego and then fills him with divine truth. But if he lets his mind take over, discussing and deciding what is to be done, he will be in danger of losing touch with the divine force. Then the lower energies will begin to act for themselves and will lead to his confusion. A simple offering of the self to the divine, devoid of egoistic motives, brings immediate results. Yet during this process the aspirant does not renounce the world and abandon his duties. He lives in the world, but he lives like the lotus, which, though rooted in mud and supported by water, blossoms in air and sunlight.

Obstacles in Meditation

Rudolph M. Ballentine, M.D.

For each person the obstacles encountered during the practice of meditation are different; for some people they are social, for others, physical, while for others their obstacles are primarily emotional.

Probably the first and most obvious problem that one will encounter is a physical one. "I have a headache . . . I feel terrible . . . My stomach is upset . . . My back hurts . . . so I can't do meditation." Another problem is with regulating the breath—not as commonly recognized as other physical problems, but important. Thoughts are also an obstacle. "I can't control the thoughts. . . . Too many thoughts come into my head. . . . I don't know how to handle all these thoughts." People become defensive if you say they have "mental problems," though, of course, all of us do. Perhaps it is better to say "problems with the mind," problems with regulating, controlling, and directing the flow of thoughts. Some people also have difficulty in developing a clear enough idea of where meditation should lead. They are not sure how to find a direction to follow during their meditation. Then there are problems which we think of as psychosocial: "I wish I could do meditation, but my husband thinks it is ridiculous, so I just can't," or "I really want to try meditating, but when you have three kids, you know, it just isn't possible." Or, another complaint, "I know it is important, but my job takes up all my time and I never have any left." Then there are emotional problems, which become obstacles for many people.

Finally dietary problems should be mentioned: there are often problems with regulating one's daily schedule in such a way that there is a time when he physiologically feels like meditating. One doesn't feel like meditating when he's starving to death; all his thoughts will be on food, he will "meditate" on food. At the other extreme, it's very difficult to do meditation after just having put food in the stomach. In this case one's consciousness is in the belly—at least it *should* be in order to properly digest the food. Since this is the grossest or crudest level of functioning—the physical material—the obstacles created here, for instance by overeating, are the most cumbersome. But at the same time they are the most obvious, the easiest to understand, and the simplest to correct.

Obstacles Arising From Dietary Habits

If the body is occupied with digestion, it is difficult to do meditation. Consciousness has the clarity and freedom to explore within only when one's system has finished with the major part of the digestive process. It becomes important, then, to find a time when one has not recently eaten to sit for meditation. Unfortunately, many people find that if they must wait three to four hours after eating to meditate, they never find any time at all, because they never go longer than that without putting something into their stomachs. But ideally, about three or four hours should be allowed to elapse after eating before attempting to sit. One must find a time when the body is nourished but not loaded, when he doesn't feel hungry and yet doesn't feel full. The kind of food eaten is very relevant here. If something very heavy is eaten, it takes a long time to digest and it will be a longer time before one regains maximum clarity and alertness. If one eats heavily consistently, he will probably never feel like meditating. A little knowledge concerning which foods digest quickly and soon leave one ready to do meditation, and which foods take a long time to digest, allows one to plan. This is a practical matter and an understanding of what happens after different kinds of foods are eaten is very useful.

Juices take the shortest time to digest. As far as solid foods go, fruits digest most quickly. If one eats a meal of fruit, within two hours he will usually feel empty again, unless he eats a tremendous quantity. But if most people eat their usual bulk of food in fruits, the stomach will be empty within approximately two hours. Vegetables, like salads, are digested a little less quickly. Next come cooked vegetables, of which one will take a much larger quantity, because they are cooked down, condensed, and become heavier. They will ordinarily digest somewhat more slowly than salads. Grains can take quite a bit more time.* After grains come protein foods: cheese, meats, legumes, or nuts. The last thing on the list is fats, because fats take a very long time to digest. If anything on this scale is eaten with fat added to it, the time can be doubled. In combining foods the picture becomes much more complicated. Emotional upsets, tension, and one's state of mind all affect the digestion. Moreover, many people actually eat more when

---

*This depends a great deal on the person. These are relative times which are approximately accurate for most people. One's digestive capacity and hunger can have a great influence. Quantity is also extremely important.

they are nervous, while they are actually able to handle less.

With this rough idea of the relative length of time it takes for different foods to be digested, the intake of food can be regulated in such a way that one will be physiologically ready to do meditation at a time when he is otherwise free to do so. If one has his whole schedule arranged to do meditation at 10:30 at night and then upon sitting down he is so full of food that he falls asleep, his efforts are wasted.

Aches and Pains as an Obstacle

The next kind of obstacle that we will encounter is on a less gross level than food but still has to do with the physical body. This set of problems is based on physical aches and pains. These are very common problems. Most people who have attempted meditation have, at some point, encountered such a difficulty. If one sits down, closes his eyes for a moment, and focuses on his breathing, he can survey the body, starting with the head and proceeding down, and will find that there are parts that feel uncomfortable. This is a problem because as soon as one sits down and the ache or pain comes into focus, it pervades one's consciousness, and occupies the stage of the mind, so to speak. Upon opening oneself to see what can be perceived in the inner world, all that comes into awareness are these red lights flashing "pain." So the usual tendency is to get up, move around, and try to forget the discomfort. The result is a harried, frenzied sort of behavior.

Trying not to be aware of the discomfort that one has makes it difficult to be open and sensitive to the world within. A systematic approach to meditation must concern itself with what to do about aches and pains. Over thousands of years, traditional practices have been developed to deal with this. The major technique for learning how to eliminate physical discomforts is hatha yoga. This includes strengthening and stretching muscles, deep relaxation, cleansing, and strengthening the nervous system through breathing practices. The hatha yoga positions are called *asanas* in Sanskrit. *Asana* means "easy" or "comfortable." The purpose of the hatha yoga asanas is simply to enable the student to assume an easy, comfortable posture and develop a supple, relaxed, physical condition so that he might sit down without the distraction of aches, pains, or cramps. The culture postures are designed to prepare one for the meditative asanas. They systematically loosen and strengthen the body so that it can assume a proper meditative position. If one has discomfort when he sits, physical postures which will help relieve that should be investigated. Muscles must be stretched and strengthened so that the body can be restored to equilibrium. It is important for such a student to experience various exercises and postures so that he can select those that seem to fit and benefit him.

The next thing is to choose correctly the meditative posture itself. Even if one is in perfect health, is relaxed, and his body is very supple, if he sits in an awkward posture to do meditation he will soon feel aches and pains. If, for example, one sits with his head too far forward, all the muscles in the back must exert themselves in order to prevent its falling forward. These muscles overwork in such a way for a while, but eventually they begin to go into spasm and to cramp.

For such reasons the ancient teachings set down very

specific instructions on the correct meditative postures. The meditative postures are those where no strain is required to keep the body in an erect position. In other words, there is complete balance. This means that the masses of weight of the body should be distributed around its axis in such a way that very little effort is required to maintain the posture. The head, chest, and hips are the three major masses of body weight. They should be arranged one above the other so they are balanced and so the spine can serve as the central core of support for them. When there is poor alignment, muscles must overexert, and tension and discomfort will result. Though one may manage to ignore the results of such poor posture because of the preoccupations of his everyday life, when he sits for meditation he will suddenly become aware of them. The problem seems magnified because one's preoccupation with the outside world is cut off as he turns his attention inward. Through surveying himself, he suddenly becomes aware of how poor his posture is.

The spine should be in the proper position: there is a curve inward at the neck and at the lower back, and there is a curve outward where the shoulders are. The spine is not precisely straight, like a rod; rather, there should be this slight curve. When it is properly aligned in this way, the head, chest, and hips are balanced one above the other. (Westerners often find it necessary to place a cushion under the hips to get the proper positioning of the spine if they sit on the floor. Some persons may have more success by sitting in a chair, which allows the back to be kept comfortably erect.)

Success in proper posture comes with constant experimentation. One must sit for some time and observe what happens when slight adjustments in position are made. As the correct posture is approached, one feels more alert and the mind becomes clearer. Often shifting position only a fraction of an inch will result in an increase in clarity of consciousness. If one assumes the best possible position each day, relaxes in it, and gradually extends the amount of time it is maintained daily, then his capacity to sit will grow. Meanwhile strength, balance, and a feeling for correct alignment increase.

Once the body is relaxed and one is seated in a good posture, one becomes aware of the breath. If the breath is jerky, it can become an obstacle. This is probably a problem in meditation much more often than is realized, because many people are still preoccupied with aches, pains, and postural balance, or because their consciousness is still too clouded by digestive overwork to allow them to become aware of the breath. Some people are jerky breathers, some chest breathers, and some hold the breath intermittently. The first step in approaching problems with breathing is to observe one's own customary pattern of breathing.

Poorly regulated breath can be very distracting. Breathing can be an obstacle or it can be a tool, depending on whether or not one learns techniques for working with it. It can be a tool that will help in eliminating and controlling other obstacles, especially emotional problems. Many people encounter difficulty in meditation because of their emotions. Emotional turmoil stirs up one's entire physiology. When one becomes emotional, the breath becomes irregular. This in turn affects many other systems. Food cannot be properly digested. Tension develops and aches and pains are accentuated. Loss of emotional control reflects on the physical, mental, and energy levels, especially the last. The whole flow of energy or prana in the body is disrupted.

Emotions are "felt," though not in the same way as senses such as taste, touch, or smell. Rather, there is a feeling of intensity in different parts of the body. Emotions create in the heart area, especially, a concentration of energy and awareness. The flow of energy in the body thus shifts and can be totally disrupted and disorganized by emotional turmoil. When this occurs, the energy is not only stirred up, it is also expended.

With anger, for instance, energy is rapidly dissipated and wasted. It is as though it were poured down a drain. Extreme anger will often be followed by shakiness, weakness, and lethargy. In one burst a person's energy can be discharged, leaving him depleted. After this, one's meditation will be disappointing. One's mind may return to his anger and to retorts he should have made ("Next time I am going to remember to say . . ."). Then the anger returns and increases, and more energy is lost. Or, if one manages to get his mind off the anger, he is likely to fall asleep because of the exhaustion that follows the upset.

In order to avoid having an emotional situation get out of control, one can work with the breath. Breath and emotions bear a very close relationship to each other. It may be impossible to say whether the breathing difficulty causes the emotional turmoil or whether the emotional turmoil causes breathing difficulties. In a sense, both are the case, because they function in an interrelated way: so when the emotions get out of control, then the breathing gets out of control, but if control of the breathing is re-established, then the emotions are calmed down; or if one can reestablish control of the emotions, then the breathing calms down. Although control of the emotions may seem difficult, regulation of the breath is direct and simple. All that is necessary is to observe the breathing pattern, to find out how it is irregular, and to return it to regularity. This doesn't mean one should eliminate emotions—they are a useful part of the personality. Just as controlling the diet doesn't mean fasting, control of the emotions doesn't mean having none.

Next we should mention those obstacles that are usually thought of as psychosocial, or as problems with other people. Most problems that we encounter with other people are really not problems with others, they are problems in us and reflect our inability to regulate ourselves. So we choose someone outside as a target to blame, such as our children: "I just had a terrible time with the kids all day. By the time it's evening and I can do meditation, I am just exhausted." This issue is related to emotions and breathing. Coping with our children can be exhausting or exhilarating, depending upon our attitude toward them. We will find in our personal experience that there are some kinds of work where the more work we do, the more energy we have. There are other situations where we feel exhausted after a few hours. Determining which occurs is not so much a matter of the muscle power used, or the number of brain cells operating; it has more to do with our reasons for acting, and what it means to us. One attitude toward work leads to a state in which we can sit down and slip easily into meditation. Another attitude will lead us to a state in which any attempt at meditation ends only with sleepiness and frustration.

When the body is comfortable—free from aches and

pains and is not overloaded with food or complaining with hunger—and once the breath is regulated, a new set of obstacles becomes apparent: these have to do with annoying, persistent, and distracting thoughts. What to do with thoughts? Many students of meditation rank as their major obstacle "trouble thoughts." How can these be handled? What is to be done with them? If he calms down the body and makes the breath regular, the student begins to find himself aware of only thoughts, and he begins to wonder what else he could be aware of; after all, isn't the mind simply a flow of thoughts? If one is to limit himself to this inner world of endless and often monotonous thoughts, how can he be anything but bored?

This raises a question occasionally asked by students: "Where is meditation supposed to lead, anyhow? What direction should it take?" We must deal with this question before we can understand how to cope with thoughts. Most of us tend to think of ourselves as more or less identical with our minds, with the set of mental habits that comes into prominence when we sit quietly. At the same time, of course, it is this set of mental habits which limits us, confines us, and prevents our growth and personal evolution. The basic purpose of meditation is to help us step beyond this circle of thoughts, to escape the repetitive chain of mental events that has us trapped. "What? Stop thinking? Impossible!" This is our initial response to the proposition. Our identity *is* our thoughts, so the idea of going beyond them seems strange. Yet the purpose of meditation is to expand awareness beyond the limits of "thinking," enlarging our field of awareness to include other nonverbal, "nonmental" areas of consciousness. Thoughts do not disappear. They remain active and visible in one corner of our consciousness. But they cease to be the totality of our awareness. Our choices and our creativity are multiplied and enhanced by escaping the limitations of our thoughts.

So meditation should lead beyond the "mind." When one grasps this, he suddenly becomes aware of the difficulty in carrying it out. "Am I going beyond my thoughts?" he thinks busily, or "I'm not going to think about that, I'm not going to think about anything. . . ." So the student realizes with exasperation that he is simply thinking about not thinking! It seems an endless cycle. It's like quicksand, in which every attempt to push oneself free only results in sinking deeper.

It is for this reason that students are often prescribed a sound on which they can focus. This, when properly selected by the teacher, permits them to turn their attention to something which is outside the circle of thoughts, a sort of "place to stand" in the inner world, from which the thoughts can be surveyed without being entangled in them. This sound focus, which is used almost universally in meditation, is called a *mantra* in Sanskrit. The task of the student becomes one of holding the attention on it and avoiding the tendency to slip back and lose himself in thought.

Once again, the breath becomes very important, since each time the flow of breath is interrupted, one's attention is jostled and shifts. If the breath is perfectly smooth, concentration can be held on the mantra and consciousness can rise to a point from which much more is included in the field of awareness. But when the breath is interrupted, so is the expanded awareness, and a jerky series of thoughts comes once more to dominate consciousness.

Over the ages, each of the obstacles encountered by humanity in its search for expanded consciousness has been identified, struggled with, and overcome. The techniques necessary for the conquest of these obstacles have been repeatedly described and taught to devoted and sincere students. What remains is only for the student to make a consistent, alert, and adventurous application of the methods. Then the obstacles gradually fade, one by one. As the obstacles disappear, consciousness rises, as is its natural tendency, toward fuller and more evolved states.

Meditation in Action

Swami Ajaya, Ph.D.

Sitting meditation and following the principles of meditation in one's activities in the world are two complementary practices that support one another. Each practice helps to deepen the other. When one practices meditation, he learns to observe his thoughts, emotions, sensations, impulses, and desires, rather than identifying with them. Action is merely a thought or desire amplified and expressed through the instrument of the physical body.

Ordinarily when one identifies with his thoughts and desires, he acts impulsively without forethought or discrimination. He does not choose whether to act or not and does not pause to consider the consequences of his actions. One benefit of meditation is to slow one down. One may feel as though a videotape were suddenly switched from fast forward to slow motion. In this condition one becomes aware of subtle inner processes that were unnoticed in the fast forward mode of everyday life. Instead of being carried along in the rush of mental events, one becomes more aware of the unfolding of these events and their sequence.

When one learns to observe his thoughts and desires in meditation, he is also creating a space between himself and his thoughts and between his thoughts and his actions. He recognizes his thoughts as being distinct from him, the observing consciousness. As a result they lose the compelling force that ordinarily carries them into action. As a result of the regular practice of meditation, one becomes aware of the space between himself (the observer) and the space or gap between a thought and its expression in action. When one is aware of that space, he is able to decide whether or not to act on the thought or to let it pass by. He will be less reactive and more able to choose those actions that will benefit him and others.

Meditation in action is an extension of the attitude and mode of consciousness cultivated in sitting meditation. The process of meditation is carried forward into one's daily life. In meditation one learns to observe his mental state while sitting quietly. In meditation in action, one continues to observe the flow of thoughts, desires, emotions, and sensations throughout the day as he is eating, conversing, walking, or engaged in any other activity. If a thought involving blame, fear, doubt, expectation, or some other emotion arises, rather than identifying with it and becoming swept along in the drama that the thought engenders, he simply notices the thought and remains a neutral observer of it. He can then consciously choose whether or not to act on that thought, rather than acting impulsively. He makes choices about whether to act or not based on discrimination. By slowing down and observing, he becomes able to interject choice. He can decide whether the prospective action will be helpful or harmful.

Meditation is not intended to be an escape from the world—rather, it gives one the means to live more effectively, harmoniously, and responsibly in the world. In sitting meditation, one creates a special circumstance to practice. In a similar way a musician withdraws to a quiet retreat each day in order to perfect his playing. Then he applies the skill that he has acquired through practice when he goes out into the world to give a performance. His practice comes to fruition when it is shared with others. Like a musician, the meditator creates a special environment to practice.* There he perfects his ability to remain free from identification with the dramas, addictions, and disturbances created by his mind. When his sitting meditation is over, he applies the skills that he has learned as he functions in the world throughout the day, and he is able to function more effectively.

Meditation is actually a special case, a controlled situation that makes it easier to learn the process of uninvolved observation. In ordinary life one is distracted not only by his thoughts but also by sensory input from the external world. In meditation one closes off sensory input as much as possible. He places himself in a quiet room with the door closed and may even wear earplugs to minimize sounds from outside. The room is dark, and he closes his eyes so that he is not distracted by the sense of sight. In this way meditators carefully create an environment free from external distraction so that they can turn their attention inward.

By creating a special situation in which sensory input is minimal, the meditator establishes a favorable environment in which he is not distracted by sounds, sights, smells, ideas, sensory pleasures, conflicts, crises, or demands from

---

*Research has shown that advanced yogis do not need a specially chosen environment in which to meditate. They learn an internal process of disconnecting their awareness from sensory input so that they are completely unaffected by external distractions. They are unaware of their surroundings even if they are in the midst of a tumult.

outside. Only his thoughts, remembrances, desires, expectations, motions, and body awareness remain to distract him. Having minimized input from the external world, he now focuses his mind on the chosen object of meditation and finds it easier to reach a state of one-pointedness and tranquility. Mental distractions may entice him and lead him to wander about in the self-created realm of thoughts, desires, and emotions. But as he perfects his practice, he will learn to distinguish between himself as the conscious witness and the melodramas created by his mind. He learns to remain at peace rather than being swept up in his mental turmoil. To some extent, this tranquil state can carry over when he steps out of the special environment he has created and confronts the world around him. The meditator can continue to observe his thoughts and emotions in his daily activities rather than losing his balance and self-awareness. Maintaining such an even state is much more difficult, of course, as one carries out the activities of the day. He is not only bombarded with his flow of distracting thoughts, but also has to confront the expectations, criticisms, suggestions, and demands of others he encounters, any of which can throw him off balance and lead him to become ensnared in and identified with all sorts of melodramas. He also confronts innumerable distracting sensory inputs that can lead him to lose his balanced state.

Psychoanalysts discourage their patients from "acting out," that is, from becoming carried away in their thoughts and emotions, allowing them to spring into action without forethought and without reflecting on the consequences of those actions. In a similar way, the meditator is discouraged from acting out in response to either internal or external promptings. This does not mean that the meditator is not spontaneous or responsive. It is important to distinguish between an open response to one's circumstances and becoming lost in the drama, for many people confuse spontaneity with emotionality.

To the extent that one is caught up in the dramas created by his mind and his environment, he is unable to act spontaneously. Instead he reacts on the basis of emotions, or preconceptions, desires, aversions, and expectations. He is not able to see a situation clearly or to deal with it in a free and open manner, because his preconceptions and habits lead him to react in a predictable, routine, and emotional way. He is not able to choose from among the many possible ways of dealing with a situation because he is identified with a particular way of perceiving and responding. There is nothing spontaneous about a preprogrammed emotional reaction. Spontaneity, by contrast, implies the ability to flow with circumstances rather than hesitating or blocking one's response, but it is not a mindless emotional reaction that can create harmful consequences. Spontaneity also implies the ability to shift one's response according to the needs of the moment, to react in a way which is open, new, and original. By developing a meditative state of mind and freeing oneself from identification with preconceived thoughts and emotional reactions, one remains open to those responses that best fit the situation. By practicing meditation in action, one learns to become responsive to the moment and to act skillfully.

Most meditators find that their most creative solutions to unresolved situations occur when they are meditating. Actually, such creative thoughts are always with us, but they are mingled with many other thoughts about past reactions, expectations, and desires. Ordinarily these latter thoughts have a greater valence, investment, or pull. One identifies with them and ignores the more subtle thoughts. But when one meditates, he learns not to be carried away by those thoughts in which he has invested, and he then becomes aware of the thoughts he has been ignoring. Often these are the thoughts that arise as a spontaneous response to the unsolved problem, and they may be of much greater value than the thoughts that one is so fond of recalling again and again. In sitting meditation one learns to ignore even the new and creative thoughts, for the goal of meditation is to go beyond all mental distractions to a state of peace and one-pointedness. During sitting meditation, one is not concerned with solving problems, but in practicing meditation in action, one makes use of those thoughts that lead to new and creative solutions and actions.

In modern society one is repeatedly taught to look outside of himself in order to find happiness. As a result, his relationships to people, objects, and circumstances are based on the conception that such relationships exist to bring him pleasure. He seeks out those from whom he expects to receive security, pleasure, or status and avoids those that he thinks will diminish those experiences. He becomes addicted to and dependent on those experiences that bring him pleasure and develops a phobic reaction to those that have been experienced as unpleasant in the past.

Most people react intensely to their external circumstances. If they receive a promotion or lose their job, or if their investments gain or lose, they may become either excited or distraught. They are affected most of all by their relationships with others. If one receives praise or approval, he feels good, but criticism or rejection can lead to feelings of self-doubt and a lack of self-worth. One can be tossed and turned in an emotional sea as a result of how others respond.

Rarely is one taught how to find happiness and fulfillment that is not dependent on external circumstances. Thus, almost everyone is at the mercy of externals. One tries to manipulate them as best he can, but they are often beyond the scope of his control. He does not recognize any alternative but to enter into identification with the multifarious dramas involved in gaining and losing. But those who embark on the path of meditation discover an alternative. They learn that there is an inner source of contentment and joy, that they need not remain dependent on external circumstances to experience happiness, that on the contrary, lasting happiness arises only when one lets go of his dependency on objects. Practicing meditation in action does not mean that one gives up his relationships to people, objects, and events in the external world. Rather, one learns to let go of his addictions and his demands that circumstances conform to his expectations. Then he becomes more open to relate to people and events as they are. While most people are preoccupied with trying to get something from others and from the world, one who has learned the art and science of meditation has experienced an abundance of joy and happiness from within. He expresses that joy in his relationships. Rather than leading to a withdrawal from relationships, meditation transforms one so that he is able to give to others rather than being preoccupied with what he lacks.

The word "love" is used in many different ways.

Someone who searches outside of himself for the objects of his desires may say that he "loves" an object or a person, but what he really means is that he stands in need and experiences the "loved" one or object as someone or something to fulfill his needs. One gives up his dependency and addictions when he matures and finds an inner source of joy. The word "love," then, has an entirely different meaning. In this case, to love means fostering the well-being of another. Instead of wanting something from the beloved, one appreciates another. The word "appreciate" means "to increase in value." One who loves enhances or brings out the best in another.

We ordinarily think that the world outside is distinct from ourselves. It appears to be there as an objective reality for us to use to fulfill our needs, but the world we seem to experience outside is really subjective. It is a mirror reflection of various aspects of ourselves. As a mirror, the phenomenal world continually reveals hidden aspects of ourselves, parts of ourselves that we deny. The world exists in order to show us our unknown and unappreciated aspects. When one becomes addicted to or demanding of another person, he is in fact desperately seeking some aspect of himself from which he has been cut off. If I cling to someone else for their gentleness, emotional sensitivity, or decisiveness, it is because they are mirroring those qualities that I do not recognize within. They are teaching me about those qualities. When I become comfortable with those qualities within, I will no longer cling to the other person. Similarly when I reject another, it is because they mirror qualities that I experience as unacceptable within me.

As one learns to acknowledge the qualities within

himself, he frees himself from the conflicts and distress that result from expectations of, and aversion to, others. Then he will be able to fully love and appreciate others, to share and to give. Meditation in action helps one to see that the world is one's mirror, and to recognize one's own qualities rather than chasing or running away from those qualities as they are mirrored in the world. By observing one's thoughts, desires, and moods, one recognizes his subtle but influential internal states and at the same time becomes less dominated by them. He becomes aware of the dramas that form from his thoughts and of the actions they manifest. But instead of being captured by his thoughts and his mirror world, he remains content and at peace within. Practicing meditation in action enhances one's awareness and leads one to master his thoughts and impulses. When one is not aware, he is at the mercy of the unknown.

There is a progressive process of becoming disentangled from the world of form and of developing an observing consciousness. Self-awareness occurs in stages. In a primitive society, what we in modern society consider to be the external world is not distinguished from oneself. The trees, forest, rivers, and heavenly bodies seem to be part of oneself. As consciousness develops one learns to view the natural world more objectively and is relatively less identified with it. Yet, as we have seen, there is still a strong tendency to identify with others. Meditation in action leads one further to objective awareness of his relationships. Instead of projecting his own qualities on another, one learns to experience the person in his own right. Finally the meditative process leads one to objectively observe his own thoughts rather than identifying with them and then acting on them to create dramatizations in the external world.

Each stage in this developmental process leads to a new level of awareness. As the consciousness of human beings in modern society is to the consciousness of human beings in a Stone Age society, so is the consciousness of the person who truly lives in a meditative frame of mind compared to the consciousness of the ordinary person in our society. Each step in objective awareness is a step toward freedom and self-mastery. There are many who idealize the primitive's experience of oneness with nature, especially when we consider modern man's awkwardness and ineptness in relating to the natural world. But becoming aware of oneself as a conscious being rather than allowing oneself to be swept up in identification with external and internal forms need not disturb one's relationship with those forms. Such awareness can in fact enhance one's relationships. What was an unconscious reactive identification can become a free, aware, and responsive relationship. Modern man is inept in relating to nature not because he is more conscious, but because he has chosen to ignore or to assert his authority over nature. One could equally choose to appreciate and enjoy the natural world experienced by the primitives as well as the innumerable aspects of the natural world unrecognized and unknown to primitive peoples.

Modern man is out of touch with nature not because of his objectivity, but because he has become identified with other aspects of the sensory world. As a result of his insecurity and dependency, he has become carried away in dramas dominated by fear, pleasure-seeking, greed, and power. As long as he believes that happiness comes from contact with sensory objects, this condition is inevitable. One frees himself from such turbulence only when he realizes that happiness is an internal state that occurs when he gives up his dependence on externals.

Ordinarily, one is seeking for what he does not have and fails to appreciate that which he has. Meditation in action is a means of cultivating awareness, which in turn leads to appreciation, and then to gratitude. In both one's relationships with people and with situations in the external world, he often feels that he is not getting what he wants. But if he were to examine each of his relationships clearly, he would find that he is getting exactly what he needs. In short, one's conflicts arise as a result of capricious and unregulated desires and their consequences rather than from external situations. If one can learn to distinguish between himself and his desires, he can learn both to appreciate and to transform his circumstances.

Every situation is a trial, a test to see whether we will become entangled and lost in reacting to it. The only reason that the external world exists is to reflect back our hidden and unknown aspects. When we fully recognize ourselves, the external world will no longer be needed and we will be free of it. Each circumstance arises to help us determine whether we will become lost in it or whether we will maintain inner balance. If one becomes entangled in a given circumstance, if he reacts with desire or aversion, addiction or hatred, he suffers. His suffering teaches him to let go of his demands and dependency, and when he lets go, his suffering ceases. After several repetitions of this round of experiences, he learns to anticipate that demands and expectations will lead to suffering, so he refrains from becoming entangled. When he is faced with an enticement or allurement, he declines becoming involved with it.

Inner turmoil and conflict arise when our desires propel us to act without regard to what is harmonious within and without. Instead of following his inner sense of balance and harmony, one allows himself to be carried away by his desires, thus creating strife. In modern society people have limited training in discriminating between their desires and their best interests. They may in some cases not act on their desires because they have been told that to do so is wrong, bad, or sinful, but that way of suppressing desires leads to an internal tug-of-war rather than to inner harmony. Meditation, however, leads one to a meta-perspective in which he is neither caught up in his desires nor suppressing them with moral imperatives. With the observing state of mind cultivated in meditation, one develops an inner sense of that which is harmonious, and he chooses to act upon only the thoughts and desires that are in accord with his inner evaluation. Acting harmoniously does not mean that one gives in to others' demands and expectations in order to avoid conflict. Instead, one finds creative and spontaneous solutions. Meditation leads one to see beyond the impasse created by the two sides of a conflict, enabling him to redefine situations so he is not stuck in conflict.

A person's insecurities usually lead him to become caught up in power struggles. He expends his energy in attempting to control others or in resisting another's control. The meditative attitude leads one to become aware of such repetitive and wasteful posturing and helps one cultivate a new way of being that frees energy to be expressed in love and joy. Having modulated desires and freed himself from power struggles, one now replaces resistance to his situation with feelings of gratitude. He now experiences an abundance of energy that can be expressed in appreciating and enhancing the lives of his family, friends, and neighbors. Instead of seeing another's need as an impingement or as an obstacle to fulfilling his own desires, he now experiences the needs of others as opportunities to share his inner wealth. Most people believe that their wealth lies in their external possessions. But the experienced meditator has found that he has a treasure within that far outshines the gold, glitter, excitement, and apparent security that can be obtained from the external world. He knows that his true wealth lies within and that, in contrast to external wealth, it is enhanced, rather than depleted, when shared. To the extent that one has learned to dive deep within and to tap his inner wealth, he replaces the focus on his desires with that of loving and giving. He seeks to benefit others rather than to take from them. Relationships with spouse, family, and friends become transformed. He now experiences fulfilling the needs of others as an opportunity for giving and is grateful for such opportunities.

In describing meditation in action, the *Bhagavad Gita* explains that one will live more harmoniously if he performs action but does not act for the purpose of receiving a reward. The ordinary person acts for what he will receive as a result; many people would not work at all if they did not expect to be rewarded. Some people hate their work or only tolerate it because they will be paid in the end. Such a person spends most of his time in frustration, complaining and feeling that his life is a drudge. He enslaves himself for the sake of the reward that will purchase a few needs or pleasures. He works because he feels that he must, so his work is poorly done, its outcome of poor quality, and little benefit is gained by anyone. If a person relates to others with a similar attitude, the results will be just as meager. If one behaves in a particular way to gain someone's favor, or sell something, or manipulate another, he, too, is working for a reward rather than giving precedence to his experience at the time of his action. If he were to attend to his immediate experience, he might become aware that he is creating discomfort, stress, conflict, guilt, and distrust for himself or for the other person. If he were aware of the subtle distress he is creating for himself and others, he might change his way of acting. But, plowing ahead toward his future reward, he remains oblivious of his dis-ease. As one practices meditation in action, he becomes aware of the discomfort he creates in himself and others, and he gradually begins to eliminate such behavior. He realizes that means and ends cannot be separated, that the means lead to like ends. If he wishes to feel comfortable and joyful, he must perform each small action in a comfortable and joyful way. Whenever he finds discomfort, he must alter his way of being rather than thinking that he can rush through the uncomfortable work or interaction in order to get to an experience that he finds comfortable. With the latter attitude, one will rarely find comfort even in situations he imagines he will enjoy and he will be unable to experience a sense of being at home with himself and his surroundings. To deal with his discomfort, he is likely to dull his consciousness through alcohol or excessive sleep.

Only when one stops looking toward the future—be it heaven, a paycheck, or a sensory pleasure—and becomes aware of his being in the moment, can genuine happiness be experienced. Happiness cannot be successfully sought. It is already here and is experienced when one gives up striving after pleasure and allows himself to experience the present.

At the beginning of this chapter, it was explained that sitting meditation and meditation in action support one another. We have seen that the state of mind cultivated in sitting meditation carries over into one's daily life, and that the same principles practiced with slight modification lead one to become more effective, creative, spontaneous, and at peace in his relationships and in everyday living. It is also important to recognize that practicing meditation in action carries over and enhances one's sitting meditation. Most of the turbulence in the mind that comes to one's awareness when he withdraws from the external world to practice sitting meditation results from the unfinished business, the discomfort and dis-ease, and the addictions and expectations that have been created while living in the world. When the mind does not have external stimuli to distract it, it ruminates on the melodramas created in past interactions with the external world. It relives those experiences and plots new chapters and endings for those stories. If one is not at peace in the way he lives before he sits down to meditate, he carries his dis-ease into the sitting meditation. Instead of focusing his mind on the object of meditation and attaining an altered and more harmonious, joyful state of consciousness, he spends his time spinning out plots. A person who lives a disorganized life will not be able to meditate effectively. In order to experience any depth of meditation, he must practice meditation in action. Otherwise he will be like Penelope in Homer's *Odyssey*. She wove a tapestry each day and unraveled it each night.

When one meditates each day, he may make some progress in calming his mind as he practices letting go of the distracting thoughts created by his involvements the previous day. When he arises from his meditation seat, he may feel more calm and serene, but he will soon become caught up in recurrences of previous dramas, and they will disturb him when he sits to meditate the next day. Each day he will take a few steps forward toward tranquility, and then a few steps back into the whirlpool of deluded thought. Many meditators live in this way, and they find that they have made little progress though they have been meditating for years.

But if one practices meditation in action, he will learn not to identify with the distractions that occur through the day. Instead of becoming lost in the dramas of his life, he will carry out those actions that are needed, free from stuggle, without becoming unbalanced, demanding, or addicted to a certain outcome. He will practice remaining at peace within himself despite whatever whirlpool exists around him. When such a person sits for meditation, his mind will already be relatively calm. There will be fewer distracting thoughts and those that occur will not have any compelling strength to carry him off. He will begin his sitting meditation already tranquil and will be able to use the special circumstance to go even deeper toward a state of undisturbed peace, inner joy, and wisdom.

Mind, Meditation, and Emotions

Phil Nuernberger, Ph.D.

Over the past twenty years or so, meditation has gained an increasing acceptance and practice in the West. While still far from being an integral part of Western society, the practice of meditation has made significant inroads in the therapeutic and medical community, and is winning increasingly broad support in business, educational, and political circles. We might say that in America, meditation has survived its infancy and is well on its way through childhood.

The reason for this increasing acceptance is that meditation has proven to be both a practical and effective tool for increasing health and happiness. The past twenty years have provided consistent clinical and scientific experience that allows us to draw some strong conclusions about the practice of meditation. In general, we can state with great confidence, based on empirical evidence, that the consistent practice of meditation leads to a healthier and more effective human being. More specifically, those who practice some form of meditation:

- have lower triglyceride levels
- achieve a lower, more stable heart rate
- have lower blood pressure
- have a slower and more stable respiratory rate
- have a more stable galvanic skin response

• report fewer psychosomatic symptoms (headaches, colds, gastric disturbances)
• take fewer prescription and nonprescription drugs
• report lower levels of anxiety and fear
• score higher on self-actualization inventories
• have increased capacity for loving relationships

The preceding describe only a few of the many substantiated benefits of meditation. In short, when compared to others who do not practice meditation, or to their own state before they began to meditate, those who consistently practice meditation are healthier, happier, and more effective human beings. Clinical experience, scientific research, and the experience of the layperson all point to one and the same conclusion: the consistent practice of meditation is probably the most important and effective self-help tool available today for personal health and effectiveness. It is also clear that under the guidance of a competent instructor, meditation can be safely and successfully practiced by almost anyone, excluding the fanatic or the psychotic, without fear of harmful side-effects.

The real question is not whether meditation is helpful, but rather how and why it works. What is it that happens during and/or as a result of meditation that yields such specific physical and mental benefits and leads to improvement in myriad aspects of one's life? The key to answering these questions lies in understanding the relationship between meditation and the emotions. The physiological, psychological, and behavioral changes listed above all reflect a more balanced and harmonious emotional state. Modern science is confirming ancient wisdom by recognizing the supremacy of mind as the determinant of health and well-being. Such new disciplines as bio-feedback, behavioral medicine, and the newly emerging psychoneuroimmunology (the study of the connection between psychological events, endocrine secretion, and changes in immune functioning) indicate that the mind is in fact a major determining factor in health and disease.

Western scientific, medical, and psychological para-digms are, however, severely limited by their emphasis on physical determinants, and have little to offer in explaining the impact of the mind and emotions on the body. From vast research experience, yoga science has provided a detailed psychological analysis of the mind and its various functions. This has been complemented by a sophisticated analysis of energy and its infrastructures within the mind/body complex. The result is a practical and accurate understanding of the subtle interactions of the emotions and their impact on the individual.

From the yogic viewpoint, we are a unique com-bination of nature, humanity, and divinity. Our animal nature is our physical structure, the body; our human aspect is our mind with its capacity for reflective con-sciousness; our divinity is the universal Consciousness that pervades mind and body. It is the successful integration of spirit, mind, and body that leads to the fulfillment of human potential. The term "animal" is not a pejorative one but simply refers to the physical structure and its basic urges. The life force, which animates the body, is chan-neled through the four primitive urges: self-preservation,* food, sleep, and sex. These urges are common to animals

---

*For a human being, self-preservation is not so much a physical preservation as it is an ego preservation, a preservation of all that I identify with being me.

and man, and they serve to ensure the survival of both the individual and the species. These drives lead us to protect ourselves from danger, to seek out food for nourishment, to give ourselves adequate rest for revitalization, and to participate in the creation of new life.

When there is deprivation or a need, energy is channeled through one of the urges and directed toward an object (thing, person, belief, action) in order to satisfy the urge. When energy is channeled toward a specific object or goal, we have what is called desire. While animals are limited in the objects that can satisfy their urges, human beings have the capacity to find many objects that can at least temporarily satisfy the basic urges. Thus, they can also create a seemingly endless number of desires. Mind, with its capacity for reflection and analysis, plays a very significant role in the selection of an object to desire. Animals, far more limited, are driven not by desire, but by their basic urges, and to satisfy their urges, will take whatever is immediately available in the environment. There is no cognitive mediation between the urge/desire/ object relationship. That does not mean that animals cannot learn (form conditioned behaviors), but it does mean that an animal is driven by its urges and not directed by cognitive activity. Thus, in yoga, an animal is seen as ruled by its nature. There is little or no capacity for moderating the urge and discriminating in the choice of objects.

It is at the level of desire that we set the conditions for our emotional responses. Depending on whether we experience the object as pleasurable or painful, the urge is either temporarily satisfied or ignored and our attention is focused on the pleasure or pain. Thus, the connection between the urge and the object is strengthened. It is as if the desire is a channel that is deepened if the object is experienced as satisfying to the urge. Every time this happens the probability is increased that this particular channel for the urge will be utilized again. In other words, the desire is strengthened. As the channel deepens (as the desire grows stronger), we become more and more attached to the object. In time, we become dependent upon that particular object to satisfy the desire. At this point a very strong *habit* has been conditioned into the personality at the level of desire. Both pleasure and pain determine the strength of the connection, or desire. With repeated pleasure, the individual develops an *attachment* to the object; if pain is the outcome, the individual develops an *aversion* to the object. We find that pain is often a more intense conditioner than pleasure. For example, one will often find that more time and effort is spent in avoiding something than is spent in attaining something.

What we have come to recognize as emotional disturbances lead to physiological changes that are disruptive and dysfunctional. These emotions create imbalances in the mind and body so their experience is called negative. Negative emotions are created when desire is unfulfilled, blocked, or somehow threatened or interfered with. The urge is left unfulfilled, the energy directed toward the object is incomplete and distorted, and we experience a mind/body disturbance. For example, when someone or something prevents us from obtaining the object of our desire, we become angry. Mind and body are out of synchrony as the vector of energy is distorted and displaced from its object. The result is a state of stress.

It is not necessary for the object of our desire to be

external to us. For example, in order to enhance (protect) our ego (self-preservation) we may harbor the desire to be boss. Yet there may be other stronger desires, such as the desire for free time, which is counter-productive to doing what is necessary to be boss. By fulfilling the stronger desire, which strengthens that desire, we frustrate the other desire to be boss. The consequence can be constant frustration, a constant low-level (and most often unconscious) state of stress and dissatisfaction, possible envy of others who achieve bossdom, and a persistent negative feeling about oneself. As long as we remain attached to the desire to be boss, we continue to frustrate ourselves, distorting our energy flow and creating disturbances for ourselves.

It is important to realize that the source of emotional disturbance is not the primitive urge, or even the desire or the object. It is, rather, our *dependency on* (attachment or aversion to) the object that leads to the distortion. When we need a particular object to feel satisfied, secure, complete, fulfilled, happy, or to have any positive mood, then we are subject to emotional disturbance. When that object is no longer available in the way in which we have come to depend upon it, we become disturbed. If the disturbance continues long enough or with sufficient intensity, the emotional energy distorts our physiological processes, and we create disease.

There is another subtlety here that is important to understand. All material objects, including thoughts, beliefs, and people, are undergoing change. The one universal characteristic of the material (phenomenal) world is that it is in a constant state of flux. Thus, if we become dependent upon an object, such as a way of being, a belief system, another person, or any other object, we are inherently insecure. At some level of the mind, there is always the recognition (albeit unconscious) of the on-going flux, so there is an unconscious recognition that the things we are so dependent upon, including our minds and bodies, are going to change. Ultimately this unconscious recognition is the root of our most primal fear, the fear of death.

The major difficulty is that our dependencies are habits, formed and strengthened in the unconscious mind. What we normally experience at the conscious level are the consequences of more primitive urge/desire/object connections formed in our early years. These connections form intricate emotional complexes in the unconscious that literally command our behavior. By the time we are conscious of our emotion, we have already disturbed ourselves. We have little or no choice as to whether we experience the emotion. By the time we are conscious of the emotion, it is already in bloom; our minds and bodies are already altered and influenced by the distortion.

This brief description of the primitive urges, desires, and negative emotions provides the background for the yogic analysis of suffering, which is intimately connected to our negative emotional states. With the concept of the *kleshas* (afflictions), yoga science provides an astute five-fold analysis of suffering. According to this analysis, we create our own suffering through:

> *ignorance* (avidya—the misapprehension of the true nature of things)
> *ego* (asmita—the false and material sense of I-ness)
> *attachment* (raga—dependencies built on pleasure)

aversion (dvesha—dependencies built on pain)
fear of death (abhinivesha—the primal fear of non-being)

From the yogic perspective, the source of all suffering is ignorance. This word, "ignorance," does not mean dumb or unlearned—it means to ignore, to be unaware of, to be unconscious. On a spiritual level, we are ignorant (unconscious and unaware) of our spiritual identity. We remain unaware of the Divinity within, and as a consequence, we maintain a limited sense of I-ness, or ego. We do not experience ourselves to be unlimited, eternal, and omnipotent, but instead experience ourselves to be the finite, limited, mind/body complex we call a personality. Thus, we become subject to the limitations of this material ego.

Even on this mundane level, ignorance continues to be the source of suffering, for it is ignorance that enslaves us to the habits of the personality. It is well known in both the East and West that man is a creature of habit. What we call the personality is nothing but a patterned configuration of habits. Habits are the basic structuring process of the mind. In more formal terms, we can define a habit as an unconscious organization of behavior to achieve a certain end. Our habits may be mental (perceptual/emotional), physiological (such as muscle patterns of tension or vascular reactivity), or behavioral (such as eating and driving habits).

The conditioning (learning) of habits is based on pleasure and pain; thus, they form the basis of our attachments and aversions. It is, then, our habits that give shape to our dependencies. Our emotional energy is channeled by the habits we have formed throughout our life. The habits that have been formed in the unconscious are those that dictate the nature of the personality.

While Western psychology, particularly behaviorism, has made intensive study of habits and conditioning, it has overlooked the most elementary fact regarding habits. Since a habit is an unconscious organization of behavior, what happens when the habit is made conscious? The answer is so simple and so powerful in its application that it seems almost revolutionary to the Western mind: when a habit is no longer unconscious, it no longer has the power to command the behavior. In other words, as long as we remain ignorant or unconscious of the habit, as long as it remains in the unconscious domain, the habit controls the target behavior and dictates our personality. The moment we become conscious, and aware of, the habit complex, however, the habit is amenable to modification or elimination. While we remain ignorant and unconscious, we have no choices to make; thus we have no control. When we become conscious, we already have the capacity and power not to behave as dictated by our habits.

To be conscious means to have a direct experiential awareness of the ongoing event. This does not mean a merely intellectual understanding. This awareness is a perceptual event, not an analytic process. Partial awareness means partial control and thus potential conflict. Complete experiential awareness means complete control. Biofeedback is an excellent example of this principle of awareness with control. Many people, including professionals, mistakenly believe that with biofeedback they will learn how to regulate certain physiological functions, such as blood flow and muscle tension. The fact is that they already control their bodies. As individuals, we are constantly and masterfully regulating, altering, and controlling both body and mind. The difficulty arises in the fact that this is done in the unconscious mind and is thus regulated by whatever habits we happen to have developed as we grew up. What biofeedback does is to make us aware of those physiological behaviors. As we increase our awareness of our internal events, and the previously unconscious mental events associated with these internal physiological events, we gain conscious control, taking the power away from the habit. Thus, we gain greater choice, create more helpful habits, and eliminate those that are not helpful.

Finally, there is the primal fear of death. Any organization is resistant to change, whether it is a corporation, a government agency, a personality, or a habit complex. Our sense of I-ness, or ego, which is built on a mind / body complex that is constantly undergoing change, is the source of our fear of death. No matter how ignorant or unconscious we remain, somewhere deep in the mind is the recognition of change, decay, and death. Thus, there is always present, though nearly always unconscious, the insecurity generated by the unconscious knowledge of change. As long as we remain identified with the personality, we will necessarily suffer this insecurity, the fear of death (change). Such constant insecurity serves as the wellspring of our other fears. It is only through the elimination of ignorance, by the direct experience of our eternal Self, that we can free ourselves from identifying with the material, limited self, and thereby become free from the fear of death.

So it is our ignorance, our lack of awareness, and nothing else, that is the source of our suffering. The problem then is not one of changing ourselves, but rather one of eliminating our ignorance. In other words, if ignorance is the source of our suffering, then becoming more conscious is the source of our salvation. It is this very power to increase our conscious awareness that makes meditation so powerful a tool in the transformation of our personality.

The Power of Meditation

The power of the meditative practice to transform the personality is direct, but very subtle. Meditation is simply the art of concentrated inner awareness. It is this dual aspect of concentration and awareness that is so effective in bringing about change. These two, inner concentration and awareness, are equal parts of one process. The greater the power of inner concentration, the more profound the inner awareness. The more profound the inner awareness, the greater the degree of freedom and balance, and the less energy is spent on misdirection and suffering: the less energy is wasted on disturbances, the more energy there is available for concentration. So when meditation is practiced correctly, it becomes a self-perpetuating tool that builds freedom and harmony.

If we have understood that ignorance is the source of our suffering, we can now understand how meditation—inner awareness—alters our suffering. Ultimately, by expanding our awareness to such a degree that we directly experience our universal consciousness, our spiritual identity, we eliminate ignorance completely and free ourselves from our self-imposed suffering. To achieve this depth of penetration of conscious awareness we are totally dependent on our capacity for concentration, for it is concentration that allows us to penetrate the veil of mind so we can enter the superconscious state.

The following analogy will help clarify how this can occur. Imagine that we have before us a bed of sand of some depth, beneath which lies hidden a very precious jewel. We wish to penetrate the sand and recover the jewel beneath. Our only instruments to accomplish this consist of a garden hose attached to a large sieve; the water coming from the hose must pass directly through the sieve. We want to use the force of the water to move the sand. The problem is that, although there is sufficient force in the water coming out of the hose, by the time the water is passed through the thousand little holes of the sieve, the force of the water is dissipated. Thus, the water has little power to penetrate or move the sand; it can only disturb and rearrange the surface, and the treasure remains hidden beneath the sand. If, however, we were to close all the little holes except one and could simultaneously increase the force of the water entering the sieve, the force of the single stream of water hitting the bed of sand would become quite significant. This increased force would allow us to penetrate the bed of sand and flush it from the jewel below. We could then direct that force to uncover more and more of the treasure beneath the bed of sand.

Our minds are like this: a bed of sand filled with thousands upon thousands of grains, some of which are known to us but most of which lie below the surface. The normal attentiveness of our conscious mind is like the sieve. Our energy, our capacity for concentration, like the flow of water, is dispersed by a thousand habits and attractions that dissipate our concentration and thus our will. There is no possibility of penetrating the unconscious mind when our concentration is dissipated, so we remain on the surface of our potential, unable to command and control the power of the mind. Moreover, those habits, desires, and fears that create mental and physical disturbance continue unabated and unregulated.

As we practice meditation (and all the supporting disciplines such as proper diet, exercise, and constructive attitudes), we are slowly learning to plug the holes that drain off our energy and capacity. First we learn to pay attention to an inner focus point, such as the breath. As we do this, we become sensitive to any harmful breathing habits, such as pauses and jerks in the breath pattern, and we simply correct them. As we refine our capacity to pay attention, we become more and more expert at concentration on an inner point such as a subtle sound or mantra. As we practice inner concentration, we slowly become more sensitive to and aware of the habit patterns in our mind and body. As we become more conscious, we are more able to perceive the relationship between our thoughts and emotions, between our emotions and our physiological responses, and to understand the consequences of our perceptual structuring. In other words, we slowly become aware of how we subtly (and not so subtly) react to events in our life, and, most importantly, we recognize the consequences of these inner reactions. As a result, we can begin to make more effective, less destructive choices—we simply choose more functional behavior.

This, in turn, leads to increased mental and physical harmony, which, in turn, allows us to increase our power of concentration. The great amount of time, effort, and energy spent previously on maladaptive habits and patterns of behavior is now available for more constructive usage. For example, when we are worried or fearful, and as a consequence maintain excess muscle tension in the neck and shoulders, we utilize energy both to sustain the disruptive emotion, and to maintain the dysfunctional muscle tension. Freeing one's mind from such worry and releasing the muscular tension allows more energy to be utilized for other more helpful and constructive activities. If we are not sensitive to the worry, or to the muscle tension, we have no choice as to whether or not to release the energy involved with maintaining those activities of mind and body. As we become more aware of our inner realities, more sensitive to who we are (that is, less ignorant), we are more able to discriminate between cause and effect relationships. We become more aware of how we have been creating disturbances for ourselves, and we simply stop creating them.

As we refine our concentration, we are able to penetrate deeper into the veil of the mind. When concentration becomes so refined as to become effortless, one-pointed, and uninterrupted over an extended period of time, we achieve a state of meditation. In this state of meditation, we become aware of that level of mind that is free from any conflict, and we begin knocking at the door of spiritual awareness and identity. When we experience this, our self-acceptance increases immeasurably, our emotions come under our control, and we experience inner peace and harmony on both the physical and the mental levels. We are more confident and secure, more able to choose our responses instead of reacting emotionally out of our old habits. In our external relationships this is reflected in greater acceptance of others, in enjoyment of life itself, and in an increased capacity for loving.

When meditation has become refined, and we achieve the ability to channel all of our expanded capacity and energy to a single point, referred to in yoga as the bindu, we are able to pierce the veil of mind and to consciously experience our spiritual identity, the Self eternal. From this vantage point, we continue to refine our capacity until all fears, worries, and doubts are resolved, full Consciousness is achieved, and we fulfill our human and spiritual potential.

Meditation and the Conscious Mind

As we have seen, the power of meditation to bring about personal growth and development is directly due to its effectiveness in increasing our inner awareness and eliminating our ignorance. This increased awareness gives us greater self-control by making our normally unconscious habits a matter of conscious choice. This allows us to make more effective choices for ourselves, and to resolve our attachments and aversions. By understanding some key consequences of an expanded awareness, we can more fully understand why our choices become more effective.

While the major determinants of personality lie in the unconscious, it is the conscious mind that gives expression to these patterns. Our conscious mind is our instrument for the expression of our ego. While it is true that it acts in service to the unconscious, it does so only because of ignorance. Its real capacity and power lies in the depth of awareness available to it. As the instrument of expression, it serves as the guardian, or watchdog, for the unconscious. As such, our conscious mind sets the conditions for the strengthening or weakening of the habits in the unconscious.

Thus, the conscious mind has a decision-making capacity that is increased with awareness. There are three interrelated tools that facilitate this decision-making. They are concentration, discrimination, and will. We have already seen that concentration is an integral part of the meditative process. It also is an important aspect of discrimination and will. Without concentration, the mind's power of discrimination, which is a subtle skill, is not brought into awareness. Concentration is also an integral part of our will, the capacity to do what we want to do. In fact, concentration is germane to almost all aspects of our life. One can have no success in life unless one has some degree of concentration. The practice of meditation (inner concentration) leads to the development of this essential skill of the conscious mind.

Discrimination is the ability to accurately perceive cause/effect relationships. There are various degrees and grades of our capacity to discriminate, and our reasoning abilities are in part rooted in our power of discrimination. This subtle capacity of the mind is the source of intuitive knowledge, and in yoga science is considered to be the source of all knowledge. The practice of meditation expands our conscious awareness of this subtle inner skill and provides access to the vast reservoir of knowledge.

Our decision-making processes are dependent on accurate knowledge and clear perception. Emotional disturbances distort our perceptions and interfere with our reasoning. When our minds are dissipated and noisily busy with the surface distractions, our decision-making process is interfered with, and we become less effective. But as we calm our mind through development of our meditational capacity, we more capably utilize our powers of reasoning, tap our discrimination, and become far more effective in our decision-making. Needless to say, developing such skills does wonders for our self-confidence.

Our capacity to utilize will also increases as we practice meditation. We can define will as the ability to consciously marshal and direct our energy and capacities to accomplish our goals. A truly one-pointed mind, a concentrated mind, is capable of tremendous will, and is thus capable of accomplishing anything. Our limitations are the limitations of a weak will. What makes our will weak are those things that dissipate our energy and attention. Emotional disturbances such as fears and inner conflicts are a major source of dissipation.

When desires conflict and the mind is divided, the force of our will is weakened. When we are negative and fight against something, our mind is divided by the negativity, and we weaken our will. When we do not complete or finish what we start, we weaken our will. When we are ill or unhealthy, our energies are depleted, and will is weakened. When we feel hopeless and depressed, our will is severely weakened. When we tell ourselves "I cannot," our will is still further weakened.

But we strengthen our will when we do the opposite of all the things that weaken us. When the mind is concentrated, when it is joyful and content, when we are positive and working *for* something, when we regulate and direct our emotional energy, our will force becomes more and more powerful. Meditation strengthens our will in many ways: by bringing about emotional stability, by increasing our self-acceptance, by intensifying our powers of concentration, and most importantly, by reminding us of our spiritual identity and opening the power of that realization for our conscious use.

The benefits of meditation do not come easily, nor does transformation occur quickly. Meditation itself is very simple; it is, in fact, simplicity itself. However, accomplishing this simplicity is quite difficult, and requires persistence, practice, and patience. A consistent and effective self-training program is a necessary prerequisite for a successful meditative practice. In self-training, one should not accept others' suggestions based on their experience as the basis for one's decision. Instead, one should seek to discover one's own inner reality through directing and examining one's own experience. In this way one gains self-confidence and develops the power of will— the ability to discriminate, to decide, and to carry through that decision in thought, speech, and action. Self-training involves all aspects of one's life, from self-study and relaxation to diet and exercise, and to the regulation of the four primitive urges.

The purpose of self-training is to develop the self-confidence that comes from self-knowledge and self-control. The entire self-training program is directed toward facilitating the meditative process and toward gaining knowledge and control of the whole of the mind. When we increase our capacity to consciously direct our mind, speech, and actions, and when we no longer create inner conflicts through indecisiveness, we can then control and direct the flow of emotional energy and achieve balance.

One final step is the deliberate practice of positive emotions. There are a number of ways we can regulate emotional energy, such as establishing proper diet and regular sleep habits, moderating our sexual activity, and systematically cultivating the proper attitudes, such as those represented in raja yoga (the *yamas* and *niyamas*). Meditation is the most powerful tool for transforming negative emotions and bringing about greater choice and freedom. The practice of meditation leads to the expression and practice of positive emotions, and it is through the expression of positive emotions that harmony comes into our lives. Positive emotions are so named because their expression brings balance and harmony to mind and body as well as to one's external life. As negative emotions lead to dysfunctional physiological processes and distorted perception, positive emotions bring about a balanced physiological response and clear perceptions.

While negative emotions have their origin in the animal nature, the source of positive emotions is in the divine aspect. Both positive and negative emotions arise from desire; however, positive emotions alone arise from the desire for higher knowledge, not from the desire for objects or sensory satisfaction. This desire for higher knowledge is what leads one to explore both the external universe and the internal truth, and it can be so powerful that even the primitive urges will come under its control. The desire for higher knowledge also leads to the positive emotions of love, joy, and peace. This love is not the romantic idea so prevalent in the West, but rather the *agape* of the ancient Greeks. Such love is an expansion of oneself, an outward expression characterized by selflessness in action, speech, and thought. It seeks no reward or return, which shows that it is free from attachment and dependency.

There is another subtlety here that must be understood, and that is the power of love (selflessness) to eliminate pain. Love is, in a significant way, the antithesis of pain. When we analyze pain we understand that pain means limitation. Pain is always related to a center of identity defined by some limiting boundary. When the boundaries or limits are removed, pain no longer exists as pain. Love is an expansion, it knows no boundaries, it does not bring anything back to a center of identity. As pain relies on self-centeredness, love is a healing force that removes both limitation and self-centeredness. It opens our self-imposed boundaries, and we become universal. If we have no circumscribed limits to our self, or identity, we can create no pain for our self. By practicing *self*-less-ness, we come to experience this expansion called love.

Now recall that negative emotions are the result of our dependency upon the object of our desires. We feel we need this object, or way of doing things, or belief, or person. We need it in order to be happy, secure, or whatever. Not only do we suffer the insecurity of possibly not getting or retaining the object, but we are also relating to this object as a limited identity. This is *my* car, *my* job, *my* wife, *my* religion; all mine, mine, mine—indicating a little self, a self defined by certain boundaries, or limits. This personal relationship (ownership, possessiveness) to these objects has an inherent self-centeredness that can only result in pain. It is a small ego, a sense of I-ness that is limited, material in nature, subject to conditioning, and thus to insecurity and fear. The entire chain of events begins in pain (deprivation/ need), continues in pain (desperation/ incompleteness), and ends in pain (dependency/insecurity). It is this endless wheel of need-attachment-dependency-need that is broken by the deliberate practice of selflessness and the experience of limitless love.

Joy, the second emotion, is what we experience when we love. This experience is necessary if we are to achieve inner and outer harmony. As the practice of self-*less*-ness is the tool to bring about love, the tool to bring about joy is laughter, and it is one of the most effective techniques available for health and invigoration. Joy, as it expresses itself in laughter, is the light that illumines our path through life. Joy is cultivated by seeking another's happiness; it is never found when seeking our own.

Here is another point that must be understood. If one asks a group of people to name the opposite of life, the most likely answer is death. This is the wrong answer. The opposite of death is not life; the opposite of death is birth. Life has no opposite. It is the force of the universe that flows in various degrees and grades. It is the source of cosmic *lila*, or play. What we do with life, however, is to impose upon it our expectations, fears, desires, and other disturbances, creating complexity upon complexity, and veiling the joy from our awareness. We impose structure and rigidity upon its infinite variety and surprise. Instead of experiencing this delight, we impose our beliefs and expectations about what life is supposed to be. What laughter does is to enable us to alter our expectations, to acknowledge the absurdity of our impositions, and to experience the freedom of being in the moment.

We cannot experience joy by trying to make the world what we think it should be, but rather by experiencing life as it already is. Wishing things were different and lamenting about what "should be" or "shouldn't be" is a guarantee that we will experience life only as a misery. When we accept and surrender to life as it is (which has absolutely nothing whatsoever to do with approval or disapproval), the fullness of joy becomes our experience. This acceptance, when extended to oneself, is the basis for the third positive emotion, tranquility, or peace.

Tranquility, the third positive emotion, is closely related to love and joy. Tranquility should not be confused with passivity or apathy. It is, rather, a dynamic quality of balance and harmony. As love is the outward flowing of energy in selflessness, and joy is the experience of accepting the natural divinity of all life, tranquility is the experience we have when we know and accept ourselves for who and what we are.

We are the source of our own turmoil. The inner doubts, fears, impulses, the unconscious drives and motivations, all create an imbalance that leads to mental and physical suffering. We remain unaware of our spiritual identity and are caught in habits and patterns of the personality. The habits that make up this small self control us, and we bounce whenever and wherever the habits bounce, nearly always reacting to the world, with little capacity to consciously choose our actions in the world. When, through meditation, we come to experience directly our true spiritual identity, the personality with all its peaks and valleys no longer exerts a claim. We experience an inner calm and tranquility, a center that is secure and free of conflict. From the vantage point of this calm, unattached center, we gradually resolve our inner conflicts and unfold the subtle potentials of the deeper mind. From this center, we can consciously choose creative and fruitful actions in the world, being responsive to, but not reacting to, the ups and downs of the changing world. Awareness of this subtle part of the mind is gained through the practice of meditation.

These three positive emotions—love, joy, and tranquility—can become the channels through which our emotional energy is directed rather than directing it through the channels that result in the dependencies of attachment or aversion. While selflessness and laughter are specific and useful tools to help bring about the experience of the positive emotions, it is meditation that holds the key to transformation.

Meditation and Meaning in Life

Arpita, Ph.D.

The alarming incidence of chronic, stress-related diseases and emotional turbulence in our society has prompted scientists and practitioners to formulate a broad array of treatments in an attempt to reduce the suffering that has an impact on so many families. Numerous approaches have been developed to alleviate symptoms, but for many, problems remain and intensify. The issue is further confounded by the fact that those who suffer from the diseases of mind and body for which effective treatments *have* been devised frequently do not comply with treatments that would improve their health and contentment.

This is particularly the case when the treatment includes lifestyle change. The simple environmental, dietary, exercise, relaxation, and breathing interventions that can reduce the tendency toward depression, anxiety, cardiovascular disease, diabetes, and even cancer, for example, are frequently ignored and are often not followed by patients, even when prescribed. Psychological interventions, which aim more deeply at the individual's makeup, would improve compliance and are actually more basic to the initial source of imbalance and subsequent dis-ease. But because they are also more challenging to understand and assimilate, particularly for those who have established lifelong patterns and crystallized world views, they are also less likely to be utilized. It is often quite difficult for one to gain enough perspective to observe one's own idiosyncracies realistically or to admit the negative outcomes they create. Thus, practitioner and patient alike are frustrated in their desires to enhance levels of well-being.

Considering the availability of effective and natural preventive practices and treatments, the hesitancy of many to seek help or to follow helpful instructions is perplexing. There is obviously something more going on beneath the surface that sabotages these individuals' intentions toward happiness. There even seems at times to be some kind of attraction for misery. The fact that there is a need for stress reduction interventions and that people resist these suggests that there is one single, underlying disturbance from which both of these maladaptive tendencies may evolve.

When one considers the pervasiveness of these disorders and the corresponding noncompliance with easy treatments for them, two questions readily surface. The first is twofold: What is this basic human stress that manifests in so many different forms, and why do people not follow through with interventions that would in fact make their lives happier and less painful? The second question that arises is more practical: How does one identify and resolve that essential inner dilemma?

Holistic interventions have been shown to reduce physical and emotional disorders, but even if one eats only whole, natural foods, jogs daily, practices stretching exercises, learns interpersonal skills, understands one's debilitative self-talks, breathes diaphragmatically, and explores the unconscious themes that lead to unsettling consequences, one can still suffer from a lack of resolution concerning the basic issue of life itself. Interventions that relieve symptoms of body and mind, while leaving the core dis-ease of the spirit unaddressed, do not solve the basic human problem or relieve the deepest pain. Compliance with these interventions is pointless if one does not also apply a treatment for the real source of human distress. What is the use of practicing health-enhancing interventions if life itself has no purpose and is only a source of unhappiness? Why work hard to prolong a life that is meaningless? For a total healing to take place, one must reach deep within the innermost core of the problem, to that which creates all the surface symptoms—spiritual unrest and emptiness.

This is the existential dilemma each individual must confront and with which each must come to terms successfully if real health and contentment are to be achieved. The stress-related disorders from which so many suffer are the stirrings and outcries of one's inner self. They attempt to call conscious attention to the essential core stress of life and prompt one to get on with the business at hand of making sense of one's existence. Inner conflict creates external conflict, and until one settles the basic internal problem, no feelings of well-being are possible within or without. As long as this remains unresolved, physical and emotional symptoms of the underlying conflict will continue to manifest, despite attempts to treat them with physical and psychological interventions. Such treatments, though effective in cleansing away many maladies, do not penetrate to the source of these manifestations of illness, for disease emanates from fear and doubt, just as health springs from a well of purpose and confidence. No real lifestyle change, no characterological transformation that will allow health and peace, is possible without a radical, positive shift in world view.

The painful symptoms of stress, then, are actually manifestations of the deep, ontological distress of human existence and can be viewed as signals that alert one to this essential problem and guide the way to its solution. Were it not for the agitation and tension headaches of anxiety or the desperation and lethargy of depression, for instance, many would continue complacently on in mediocre and detrimental grooves. But the discomfort of these symptoms can force one to admit that something is askew and that change is needed. Pain is the friction caused by imbalance and misalignment, and just as with a squeaky wheel rubbing against its axle, it is a symptom that something must be set right and greased if any real peace or progress is to be achieved.

People are creatures of habit, though, and with tendencies toward fear and laziness they are hard pressed, even at great expense to themselves, to accept facts indicating errors that will necessitate change. They tend to continue on in their old patterns, and as a result they frequently resist confronting a problem until a major life-threatening disease or situation manifests. Until the wheel refuses to budge another inch or until it cracks and breaks under pressure, they will attempt to force it onward, ignoring its protests. But the time comes when one simply cannot continue any farther in the same way, and then one must face reality, for at that point the possibility of death confronts one point-blank. One is at last forced to deal with the essential issues of life: Who am I? Why am I here? Where did I come from? Where am I going?

The poignancy of the drama is that by behaving unhealthfully and by ignoring warning signals, one actually pushes oneself to this desperate point at which avoidance is no longer a choice. Confronting the issue of death is an inevitable human fact, and sooner or later we must all do it.

Until one has resolved the basic questions of life by and for oneself, identifying a purpose in life and a place in the universe, a spectre of unhappiness will overshadow every transient pleasure and haunt every silent moment. Without a personal cosmology with which to interpret life, one is like a lone traveler lost in a dark, strange, and dangerous territory without a map or a compass to guide the way. Anxiety and confusion are the natural reactions to such a dilemma, and fear or despondency are the outcomes.

We are all transient sojourners through life, but, without any sense of direction or purpose, we are mere wanderers aimlessly roaming about in a vast labyrinth. Stress is inseparable from such a predicament, for no sense of reason, worth, mastery, or security is possible under these conditions. Without some thread of continuity formed by a theme in life, the events that comprise one's existence are like scattered beads tossed about haphazardly with no design or use. When one then looks back over the years, one sees only disarray and loss rather than the ordered beauty and strength of a necklace, with each bead strung carefully along a single thread. That thread is the line that gives a discernible design to the labyrinth and provides direction, security, and the route to freedom.

The puzzle of life is apparent, and the challenge of the task is pressing, but how is this dilemma to be solved? There are as many solutions as there are people on the planet, but there are only two basic approaches to the problem: a conscious approach, or an unconscious approach. Most people select, by default, the second alternative. Many people are overwhelmed by the immediacy and complexity of the problem of individual existence, and they naturally seek out some rock to which they can play vine. In fear, they dependently cling to and identify with a person, a role, a possession, or an ideology, and in so doing acquire identity, structure, and direction. But when the foundation yields or the scaffolding folds, they are devastated and lie helpless until another host arrives to carry them further. Knowing the transient nature of things, however, these people live in fear of loss, and even in their most secure moments, their awareness of the unreliability of external objects shakes their stability. Furthermore, because they deny their own inner strength, they fail to tap their capacities or to realize their full potentials.

Others seek meaning by automatically accepting the prepared formulas provided by the society or family into which they are born. They may earnestly follow the tenets and principles described, but without some deep inner experience to validate the paradigm personally. Their adherence tends to be superficial, perfunctory, and unsatisfying in either the long run or in times of great distress. Such blind adherence to an inflexible system cannot serve as skin does to protect and contain one naturally throughout a lifetime, but instead resembles a cold, hard armor that encases one and prevents penetration from the outside. One can easily become stifled and stagnant in such a system that limits rather than liberates. By deflecting personal responsibility for their lives, these individuals forfeit the zest and immediacy of living.

Perhaps in reaction to the over-dependent mode, there

is another approach that represents the pseudo-autonomous orientation. These people avoid affiliation with any recognized approach and feign personal confrontation with the hub of existence by endlessly sampling a variety of theories and systems. They may play armchair philosopher or amateur theologian in the intellectual arena, but this approach excludes the indispensable elements of heart and commitment. Their mental gymnastics lack vitality, and they frequently fall prey to dry mechanism, cold egoism, cynicism, or isolated fatalism.

Although their social and career skills may be superb, their inner and personal lives can easily atrophy as they become more deeply engrained in their approach. They themselves may not realize what is wrong, and their efforts to single-handedly remedy their discomfort by relying more and more on their limited and isolating approach only deepens their plight. This situation points toward the human tendency to assume that the way we perceive a situation is how the situation actually is and to conclude that everyone experiences it similarly and feels the same way. Thus, if we find no workable solution, then we conclude that no solution exists, and the whole dilemma is utterly hopeless. Frustration and despondency therefore set in, and we become trapped in a feeling of helplessness from which we see no possible escape. Thus, we either curl up mournfully to await life's next sorrowful event or we pace and rage in agitation, beating our heads against the wall and shaking our fists about life's injustice.

Thus, it is not surprising that many people attempt to deal with the problem of meaning in life by avoiding it. They focus on distracting themselves in a swirl of *have to's, should's* and *want's* that keep them too busy to realize that there is no foundation or purpose beneath their actions. They are like the cartoon character who can easily tread air until he looks down to discover the chasm beneath him. The remedy they often adopt is to avoid at all costs the temptation to look down. These people constantly distract themselves from inner uncertainties by blithely looking for happiness and meaning in the external world.

They are repeatedly disappointed, of course, and so are driven to seek fulfillment more frantically through a series of goals they work to attain. First they must have a good education, then a compatible partner, an interesting career, a lovely home, a wholesome family, financial security, status, power, and so on. To further intensify the distraction, they create a series of diversions to prevent detection of their underlying emptiness. In unconscious defensiveness they quickly fly from one stimulus to another, tossed by the windy current of events. There may be a continuous stream of errands, tasks, movies, phone calls, newspapers, visits, appointments, trips, meals, discussions, meetings, purchases, parties, chores—and then there is also work. But this busy flurry of activity is only procrastination designed to put off confronting the deeper challenge of life. The internal stress is temporarily upstaged.

If it is not sufficiently camouflaged by a busy whirlwind of activities at work and home, then more potent stimuli can be administered to assist one in successfully avoiding the void. These may include such indulgences as compulsive overeating, romantic entertainments, alcohol consumption, and a wide variety of techniques designed to keep important interpersonal relationships in a constant state of uproar. Still another strategy is to make use of physical symptoms themselves as distractions. Here, one focuses only on the outcome of inner stress and not on the cause. One would rather accept physical discomfort and degeneration than look beneath the symptoms to encounter the psychological and spiritual pain below. Thus, preoccupation with the surface symptom itself becomes a defense to which we fearfully cling, and then no cure is possible.

The insulation and false sense of meaning resulting from these avoidance techniques, paired with the perpetual drama that they create, allow neither time nor inclination for one to confront the deeper issues of life. One is too wrapped up in day-to-day concerns to consider life as a whole. But as the years pass by, one is unsatisfied, and a gnawing ache deep inside, a vague lack of fulfillment, continues. In the end, when one has run through the gamut of years and has nothing of value to show for the effort, when all the days have somehow slipped away, one at last wonders, What was it all about? Even many of the great artists, philosophers, and leaders of the world who have made significant contributions to humanity have felt the weight of emptiness in their lives. A time comes when even they ask, and are asked by others, "Is that all? There must be something more! Surely there is more."

If one does not choose to confront this problem on one's own, life will often push one to do so by providing a kick that stuns one away from one's protective distractions, attachments, and interpretations. Ironically, all the common stop-gap efforts that people engage in to put off the anxiety of dealing with the existential dilemma actually lead to a life of greater stress, with emotional upset, personal stagnation, and chronic disease as the eventual outcomes. Then the irony goes full cycle, for these avoidance behaviors result in suffering that forces one to confront the very issues that one has so ardently run from: one's mortality, one's destiny, and the meaning of one's life.

Thus the avoidance of pain through resistance and defensiveness actually leads to difficulty that one can resist or defend no longer, and one must finally give up and face the reality of life, whether one is prepared to do so or not. Our balking only serves to increase the severity of the force required to get us going in the right direction. The easy way out is to cooperate and face the issue of meaning, but we stubbornly and fearfully refuse to do this.

It is apparent that looking to the external world for the solution is only a detour that cannot give happiness but that can give great unhappiness. We are accustomed to the external world, though, and the unknown inner realm is like a dark room at the top of the stairs. That is where the treasure is, but we are afraid to go there. Actually, simply deciding to accept that we must eventually ascend those stairs relieves a great deal of tension, as does acknowledging the fact that going into the dark room is in truth less painful than indulging in all the stalling that leads to our eventual despair and torment. For we really want those secret, hidden treasures, and we will not rest until we have them. We kid ourselves by denying this and by pretending to be satisfied with the world's playthings and distractions alone.

What, then, is the effective and conscious way to relieve the essential inner stress that plagues us? First, we must admit that we are not content and that the external world cannot satisfy our sense of emptiness. Then we must start looking in the only place left—within—and confront the unknown in order to gain knowledge of self and of life. Then we can develop a personal philosophy of life based on our own inner experience, and from this our purpose will emerge. The challenge of the existential dilemma is to find purpose and meaning in life, even if we have to create one for ourselves.

Lack of purpose is no excuse for misery; if we are miserable, then it is our duty to learn how to be happy, and no one else can provide this for us. This inner happiness cannot be achieved without a sense of meaning and purpose in life, for without purpose there is no direction, focus, or commitment that leads to involvement and engagement in life. Without these, every task is drudgery, and one must prod oneself through the day or the decade with the avoidance of punishment or attainment of reward as the only productive motivators.

But with a sense of purpose, one aspires toward something; one is actually drawn toward one's ideal, and energy comes from the ardor of desire in one's own heart. This creates a force that brightens the way, lightens the burden, and smooths the path. These simple equations describe the law of inertia: resistance leads to stagnation, and willingness creates energy. Willingness is the gate opener and the energizer. Simply letting go of resistance and saying yes to the challenge makes what was once a foe into a comrade. Then progress is possible.

The final touch of irony is that by facing one's plight and confronting one's finite nature—that is, by accepting the inevitability of aloneness, suffering, and death—one can actually be inspired and vitalized and can become aware of a reality beyond the mundane physical realm. In the face of loss and death, life is more vibrant and precious. It is our very impermanence, the fact that there is a deadline, that gives a thrust to time, and it is our fear of no control, of incompletion, of inconstancy that gives life its exhilarating zest. For with risk comes excitement, and with acceptance of the challenge comes engagement and a kind of peace. By viewing the situation as a kind of sport, one can learn to skillfully and joyfully ride the crest of the moment. In the midst of the tumultuous onslaught of events, one can attain the capacity to remain calm, controlled, centered, and above the roar.

Then, like a surfer, one can be held aloft by the waves and currents that sweep others away. The blows that life administers can be used either as uplifting and awakening energizers or as overpowering tormentors. It all depends on how they are perceived, for it is one's subjective interpretation that makes these occurrences into guides or jailors. In this sense, reality is what our cosmology makes it out to be. We alone have the responsibility for creating that framework for ourselves, and we have the choice of selecting either a positive or a negative world view. The mind may have a tendency to go toward the negative, but the spirit knows better. Why decide upon an outlook that is either too good or too bad to be true, and thereby set ourselves up for disappointments, when we can devise a more realistic one that can lead to happiness?

Rather than rushing through life to get away, one has merely to be still, and a way will be found. And that way is to be still. To look inside and unravel the mystery, the first step is to turn from the external. Sitting alone quietly with no distracting stimuli from the outside world will introduce one to a vast and wondrous inner world. It is that easy; but also that difficult, for there are many inner distractions. The great meditative traditions of the world, however, provide instructions for how to proceed. After withdrawing from environmental interaction for a designated period of time, one must then learn how to relax the body so that it does not create any distractions.

Finding a peaceful spot, one should sit in a steady, comfortable position with the posture straight. Regulating the breath by controlling the movement of the diaphragm will enhance physical and mental relaxation and energize the body and mind as well. When the body and mind are calm and alert, emotional balance is attained. By focusing the mind on a single object of concentration, such as a sound vibration, one can remain unperturbed by either the pleasant or the noxious stimuli that begin to arise in the unconscious mind. Focusing resolutely on the present moment eliminates disturbances from the past and future events, and maintaining a nonjudgmental observer stance to whatever flows by teaches one balance and improves emotional control. Self-awareness and understanding are also improved when this method is practiced daily over a long time. Acting in the external world also becomes more peaceful and skillful.

But how does this practice help one to develop a philosophy of life? Meditation is not inner discourse or analysis that yields a rational package of theories, but the practice of meditation certainly does yield a personal cosmology, a meaningful philosophy of life based on direct inner experience that is validated by external experiences as well. It is a conscious focusing of mind and heart so that spirit may become more apparent. When one removes the distractions and blocks, then one can see clearly.

One does not use thought or emotion to solve the riddle. Rather, the conscious mind and negative emotions must be stilled, and then that which is beyond these speaks, and one's understanding increases on a subliminal level. This side effect of meditative practice is a type of incidental but essential learning that increases one's sense of meaning and purpose. By looking within, one not only confronts thoughts and feelings, but also encounters what seems to be a void, and beyond this one discovers a wise and quiet inner teacher whose guidance is essential to solving the riddle of life. This inner teacher is one's own conscience, and to ignore it is truly ignorance. The conscience is beyond the foibles of mind and emotion, which are highly untrustworthy advisors that habitually mislead one. The conscious mind cannot help one in the inner journey, though it is an important aid in external affairs. The emotions are likewise notoriously fickle and unsettling, though their positive use is important to successful daily living.

For the journey within, however, the sole guide is the silent voice of the conscience beckoning one toward peace and fulfillment. It is that nonanalytic, nonemotional consciousness within that gives one an understanding of life. When one listens in silence and stillness, that wordless message becomes apparent and brings with it meaning and purpose that make life a song of joy and a gesture of love. With a personal philosophy, one has an interpretative framework and a sense of meaning and direction that keep one afloat in the external world and lead one to spiritual fulfillment within. That spiritual fulfillment is the sole consoler of all stress. Only then does true peace emerge and spread its soft rays outward to embrace all of life fully and without reservation or condition.

Meditation and the Unconscious Mind

Rudolph M. Ballentine, M.D.

A systematic approach to meditation helps us in studying the mind and brings about a gradual expansion and transformation of the personality. When we meditate, this growth process tends to happen on its own; it's a natural tendency of the human being. But we can either hinder or facilitate the process. We can through our efforts create the conditions to optimize the process—or rather, more precisely, we can stop creating the conditions that interfere with the process.

Assuming that we have a certain period of time that we have set aside to work with meditation, we should have a clear understanding of what steps to take to help the process occur. First, we need to have arranged our schedule, our life habits, in such a way that we're sufficiently rested: we're not sleepy, but we haven't over-slept; we're not hungry, but we're not too full; our body is sufficiently cleaned out that we can feel alert; and we are sufficiently relaxed that muscle tension does not interfere with our ability to meditate. So these are the basic conditions that we have to pay attention to: sleep, food, cleansing, and relaxation. It takes some planning, some engineering, and frequently some ingenuity to organize our schedule in such a way that all these conditions are met at the same time—a time when we really have the opportunity to sit for the practice of meditation.

Before sitting each time we should examine ourself to

determine whether we are carrying muscle tension that would distract us during our sitting. For if we have tightness and tension in our body, then part of our mind is going to be involved with that tension; such tension acts as a sandbag that weights down the balloon of consciousness that is trying to rise. Tension and tightness in our body always relates to some psychological issue. This is more obvious at some times than at others. If tension is in our arm and we've just had an argument with someone, then it's obvious what that tension is about. But often, tension is difficult to decipher, hard to trace to its source.

If we are carrying around some degree of tension that we're not consciously aware of, and we go to sit and try to focus the mind, we find difficulty in doing so—because we're trying to put the mind in a certain locus but the mind is still partly involved with whatever that tension means and is trying to express. Thus our mind is split. Meditation is the exact opposite of this—the meditating mind is the antithesis of the split mind. Therefore it's very important for us to create, insomuch as possible, a state of maximal relaxation before sitting down and attempting to meditate. We can do that in a number of ways: for example, through hatha postures or systematic relaxation exercises. We should know the techniques of relaxation, and each time before sitting we should ask ourselves, "Do I need to do some relaxation or not?" Actually, the question is more likely to be, "Do I need to do a lot of relaxation, or a little? Do I need to do some stretching, or some postures? What exactly do I need to do to release the energy that is now tied up in my muscles so that it will be free for me to use in meditation?"

After we have attended to the basic conditions and

have established a state of maximal relaxation, then we sit—and it is essential that we know how to sit properly, in a comfortable, steady, straight posture with the head, neck, and trunk aligned. After we assume our seated meditation posture, we should close our eyes and again briefly examine ourselves to make certain that our body is relaxed. Next we turn our attention to the breath, watching our breathing and seeing that it is regulated—that there are no jerks or pauses and that our breath is not shallow or noisy.

Then we turn our attention inward—not just away from the outside world, but away from the physical body. By this point in the meditative process we should have gotten the physical body fairly well attended to, so that we now have time to attend to finer degrees or grades of awareness. It's like finally having gotten the children to bed at night; now things are quiet, and we have time for ourselves. What we're actually doing is turning our attention toward that field of activity which we call the mind; what we're going to encounter is our own thought process, what our conscious mind is busy doing.

And what will that be? The mind may be saying, for example, "I wonder if my back is going to start hurting me the way it often does when I sit like this? Maybe I should change the way I'm breathing. How long am I going to be sitting here? Why am I sitting here? Is this really necessary? When I get up from here, I'm going to do such and such," and so forth. The conscious mind is going to be carrying on a thought pattern, a train of thoughts. Definitely. That is its nature.

Now, this pattern of thoughts has a certain basic quality to it—it is very *I*-oriented. "What am *I* going to do when *I* get up from here? Should *I* be sitting here? Will *my* back begin to hurt again? What am *I* going to do if *my* back hurts? *I* want to meditate. *I* have told people that *I* meditate. If *I* don't follow through then *I'm* going to be ashamed of *myself*." I, I, I. The distinguishing characteristic of what's happening in the mind at this level is that everything that's going on is related to our concept of the self. In fact, the mind is constantly bolstering and shoring up our self-image, what we think of ourselves as being—and very carefully not departing from *I* and what *I* think and what *I* typically does, and what *I*, this particular *I*, is all about.

This aspect of the mind is the ego, or *ahankara* as it's called in Sanskrit. *Ahan (aham)* means "I" and the suffix *kara* means "making." Thus, *ahankara* is literally the *I*-making part of the mind. It keeps on making this *I*, continuously making this self-image, this self-concept, this entity that we think of ourselves as being. Thus, there's likely to be a certain continuity or logical progression to our thoughts, especially if we think of ourself as being logical. (If we've learned to accept ourself as being somewhat irrational and illogical and rather flighty, then there might not be a great deal of logical progression to these thoughts, but generally there is.) So thought A in some fashion leads to thought B, which in turn leads to thought C, and we're going along being reasonable and being ourself.

It takes a certain amount of effort to do that, and therefore eventually we get tired of doing it; it becomes burdensome, and we feel as though we have to stop for a while—it's too onerous a task to continue. At which point, rather than give up our identity to which we cling so tenaciously, we decide to give up our consciousness and we fall asleep. Then we quit forging our chain of logical progression; we rest and do many other interesting things that go on while we're asleep but that, we might say, don't come to the light of day. Then we wake up and resume this A-to-B-to-C mental functioning in our very characteristic self-imaging, self-perpetuating fashion: *ahankara-ing*—going right along, busily making *I,* making *I,* making *I,* until we again exhaust ourselves with it and then fall asleep once more. How restricted our *I* is, and how much effort it takes to hold it together, keep it going, and make it acceptable to ourselves, determines how quickly we get tired and how long we have to rest to recover from the effort. If we have a relatively small, restricted, confined *I,* then we probably need a lot of sleep; if we aren't so small-minded, we probably don't need so much sleep.

When we sit for meditation our first job is thus to try to get a glimpse of this *I*-making process, to watch the process going on. What we really want to do is to disengage ourselves from that process. We don't want to try to stop it, because who's stopping it? "*I'm* stopping it, because *I* want to be a good meditator. *I* have told everyone that *I'm* going to be a good meditator, and *I'm* determined to succeed." So we're doing it, we're not stopping it.

Therefore that approach won't work; the more we try to control it, the more we reinforce the sense of *I* and the more we lock ourself into the very process that we're trying to eliminate. So we can't really stop the process—but we can disengage a certain part of ourselves from it and let it go on and observe it: observe the thought patterns, study the conscious mind. As we do that, we will find that the conscious mind begins to lose some of its usual characteristics, because there is a different sense of *ahankara* that is now coming into being, a different sense of *I* that's standing here watching—witnessing, dispassionately observing—this process.

There are various levels of consciousness; there are differing varieties of I-ness. Therefore we can say to ourselves, "Who am I? I am this person who thinks this and thinks this. But wait a minute—I can be something different, I can be that which observes this process of being *I*, that which observes this process of personal I-ness in the making. There's an *I* who's being the typical me, but there's someone else who's watching it all. That's also me."

At first this *I* that watches, this witnessing or observing *I*, is an unstable entity that quickly gets absorbed back into our habitual mind-set. But as we practice, this particular bit of *I*, this entity that is the observer, becomes stronger and able to observe more consistently.

By way of illustration, suppose our thought process is going along in typical fashion: ". . . and I had an argument with so and so today, and I said such and such, and the other person said this and that, and I know they were wrong and I was right because . . ." And the observer, watching the conscious mind and studying this thought process, says, "Hmmm, *I* is getting pretty defensive here, really trying to convince himself that he was right." That's the observer functioning at its best. But suddenly the observer says, "And you know, he *was* right, no question about it, and the other person was dead wrong." The observer has suddenly fallen out of his observer's chair down into this little train of thought. But with practice those tendencies to topple out of the observer's position are gradually reduced, and the observer part of our consciousness gathers strength and becomes more stable, better able to resist getting involved in the workings of the mind-train.

Because the I-ness at the observer's level is not so desperately trying to maintain itself, our sense of I-ness begins to shift, our self-definition starts to change. This alteration in consciousness is in some ways similar to what happens to us when we fall asleep. The consistency of our self-image and who we are begins to dissolve and dissipate, and other things start coming into our train of thought. It's no longer invariably, "*I* am thinking, *I* am remembering, *I* am doing." Suddenly there's another sense of entity, another sense of memory, another sense of impressions, and the *I* that had been tying everything together begins to disintegrate. In fact, many people actually do routinely fall asleep at this point in meditation. They sit down and close their eyes and drift off for fifteen minutes or a half hour. When they wake up they feel refreshed, and may consider that they've had a good meditation session. But really they haven't been meditating at all, they've been dreaming. Meditating and dreaming are two vastly different processes.

In our ordinary waking state, the I-ness that is our conscious mind is what prevents the unconscious, the subconscious, from coming into our awareness. That's why we're not aware of what is subconscious—indeed that's why it is subconscious instead of conscious. The subconscious doesn't fit in with our picture of who we are in our daily life. We go along throughout the day being our usual self, our accustomed *I,* and everything that doesn't fit we push out with such energy that we exhaust ourself. But when this sense of I-ness begins to fragment and dissipate, then the whole mental field begins to receive impressions from the subconscious and they come into awareness. Nothing is holding them out; they begin to come back up. One of two things must now happen: either I-ness, the sense of *I,* globs onto these *samskaras* (impressions, imprints, memory traces) and groups them into the dramatis personae of a dream, or I-ness goes higher and observes: either we meditate, which is what happens when I-ness moves up to the observing position, or we dream, which is what happens when I-ness is absorbed into the samskaras from the subconscious, producing a little play.

When we begin to dream, our sense of I-ness continues its functioning, but it starts getting caught up in the samskaras that are coming from the subconscious, grouping them and coalescing into different *I*'s, which interact among themselves, creating the drama called a dream. But all the *I*'s are only us, only fabrications of the one self. Dream therapy, which is relatively common, is essentially the process of trying to remember, in the ego state, some fragments of what we've experienced in the ego-disintegrated dream state and make inferences about what must be down there in the unconscious. Meditation, on the other hand, is the process of maintaining the observer while the ego dissolves, and observing the unconscious directly. It's more efficient. Dream therapy is superseded by meditation.

During our sitting, as the subconscious impressions begin coming into awareness, we need to develop the habit of monitoring our consciousness to make certain that we are maintaining the position of observer and not slipping into the dream state, not getting caught up in the shadow-play of our mind. When we are maintaining our neutral witnessing, the impressions from the past come up in a piecemeal, fragmented way. They come and they go. When, however, they begin to take on identities and when there begin to be struggles between this set of thoughts and feelings and that set of thoughts and feelings, then either we're daydreaming or we're dreaming, but we're not meditating.

The unconscious is filled with all kinds of memory traces and film clips of past experiences: things that we've gone through, things that we've heard, things that we've fantasized that we never experienced, sometimes things that we've fantasized in the periphery of our consciousness that we never were even aware of. These things all get salted away in that subterranean reservoir called the subconscious. Then as the ego is dissolved or temporarily melts away a bit, these samskaras begin to come back up into awareness. Because the observer is situated far from the madding crowd of our mental impressions and is not threatened by them, it can tolerate seeing things that the ego can't. Therefore the observer can allow these memory traces to come up and simply look at them and say, "Hmm, that's interesting; fancy that—who would ever have thought that was down there." That's all it ever says. It doesn't say, "Oh, what a horrible thing." That's not the observer speaking, that's the ego speaking.

Memory traces can make the ego anxious, but not the observer. The observer has nothing to lose by seeing, whereas the ego has its existence to lose by seeing, by assimilating. The ego can't assimilate. Therefore, we may sometimes have the experience of beginning to get a glimpse of certain memory traces from the unconscious, and then suddenly having the process stop cold—because our ego has become scared. The samskaras pose a threat to our ego; the ego, fearing that it may be dissolved, reestablishes itself: "*I* don't think such things. What's going on here? I don't even remember those things—what were they? I guess they weren't anything." And *I* (or rather, that particular level of I-ness) reasserts itself, reconstitutes itself, and willfully proceeds along its habitual grooves in the conviction that maintaining the mental status quo is better than tolerating all that interior disturbance.

The whole sense of I-ness is contingent on keeping the subconscious or unconscious out of awareness. That's the definition of ego. Ego is that part of the whole that we have taken, leaving the rest aside. The ego screens out, excludes, all the things that we're not able to deal with. The ego constitutes itself out of a very limited part of our total mind.

If we are systematic, regular, and persistent in our meditation practice, then gradually, progressively, the subconscious will be brought into consciousness and integrated into our personality. What eventually happens is that a new ego is formed. Actually we can look at it two ways: we can say the ego is eliminated—that is, our level of A-to-B-to-C mental functioning stops operating in its particular characteristic way—or we can say the ego is expanded. A new ego, somewhat like the old ego but now with the capacity to include, accept, and assimilate much more, is now operative as a result of the meditative experience. This is, as we've said, a natural process. For the meditative observer has witnessed the ego as well as samskaras X, Y, and Z that have come into awareness, that have been noted dispassionately, and that have been accepted as part of the self. Therefore we have ego #1 plus X, Y, Z equals ego #2, which is a new ego. It's bigger.

Now, one might feel that the ego is already big enough, but this points out a problem in our use of language, because actually the whole concept of expanding consciousness has to do with making the ego larger. The ego that is the most offensive is the one that's the smallest, the most rigid, the most frightened, the most desperate to maintain its integrity. It has the largest mass of *excluded* material; the largest unconscious.

It is only by dissolving the ego so that it can expand that we strengthen the ego and make it more healthy. The ego doesn't become stronger by becoming more rigid. Rigidity is not strength. This process of ego expansion, of personality transformation, of self-realization, continues to unfold as we persist in our meditative efforts. Ego #2 plus assimilated samskaras R, S, and T produce ego #3, which in turn gives way to an even more expansive ego #4, and so on. In this way we grow in our awareness, we expand our consciousness. Every time we take something from the unconscious and make it conscious, our consciousness has grown, our conscious mind, our conscious self, has been expanded. Our goal is to expand the conscious mind so that we have full command of ourselves and complete understanding of ourselves.

This is a very important point. Our goal is not to try to go up to some unaccustomedly high level of observation and trip on all the samskaras that we find floating around in violent technicolor, not having any idea of what to do with them or where they came from or whether they're us or monsters or whatever, and then come out of it and go right back down to good old ego #1 and exclaim, "Wow!" That's not our goal; that's called tripping. Drug experience is one way of doing that. People take drugs and become aware of vast areas of the unconscious and are exposed to all kinds of samskaras, but they don't assimilate any of the experience. The sense of ego doesn't change. They come back down afterwards and they're right back where they were. Or they aren't able to relocate their ego, in which case we put them away with a regretful sigh: "Poor guy, he took too many drugs and now look at him, he's a mess."

In meditation we're not after that kind of dramatic, sensational experience that leaves us shattered. We're after a gradual, progressive expansion of ego so that we may attain the ability to direct our energies and potentials as and where appropriate. Our goal is full self-comprehension and total self-mastery. To make progress toward this goal when we sit for the practice of meditation, it is vital that we cultivate the habit of maintaining a neutral witnessing position or attitude vis-à-vis the samskaras that arise from the unconscious. Systematic, regular, persistent practice is essential for success in this endeavor because frequently the samskaras come charged with vivid images and strong emotions. It's easy to get caught up in these surges and expend a lot of energy either defending ourselves against them or justifying them. When we find that this has happened to us, we needn't be chagrined. It definitely will happen time and time and time again. We do need, however, to learn to recognize when we are becoming involved and to form the habit of extricating ourselves and returning to our stance of neutral witnessing.

As we sit for the practice of meditation, whatever comes into consciousness—no matter how highly charged it may be—is simply to be dispassionately observed, neutrally noted, and then let go of. No matter what it is, we should not try to do anything with it. For as soon as we begin doing something with it, then we're no longer simply observing it. In daily life—in contradistinction to sitting for meditation—we often have to do something with it while at the same time trying to maintain some sense of neutral observance. That is called meditation in action, and is a different technique from sitting meditation, as indicated in chapter three.

In sitting for meditation, it is crucial that we maintain a basic noninvolvement with whatever comes up for us. For example, we may note, "Here is a memory or an image with tremendous fear associated with it. Isn't that interesting; why would there be so much fear tied up with that? Now here's another image and there's so much sadness connected with it; I wonder why?" Not "Here is an image; oh, I feel so sad," but rather "Here is an image; there seems to be sadness with the image, and when the image goes, the sadness goes."

If we are successful in learning to habituate our mind to this unattached mode of functioning when we are sitting for meditation, certain patterns in what we are experiencing will begin to become apparent. This is analysis in the true and proper meaning of the term. We begin to comprehend the workings of the mind and to understand that the subconscious has its own way of being put together, its own rules of structure. The subconscious is not like the conscious mind, and what we generally call logic is not a part of it, but it has its own structure. We can analyze both the conscious thought processes and the unconscious. But analyzing doesn't mean all of the value-colored intellectualizing that we can do with anything that comes up from the bed of memory. For instance: "I acted poorly in this situation because so and so did such and such to me when I was a child." That's not analysis, although it sometimes goes by that name. That's defensiveness, rationalizing, making excuses, trying to relieve ourself of responsibility and maintain our present ego structure.

A lot of what is so-called self-analysis, or even analysis with the help of a professional person, degenerates, without anyone's realizing it, into this sort of ego defense, sometimes into a series of ego defense mechanisms. It's a slippery kind of thing. It's easy for that to happen. (On the other hand, it sometimes happens that a person seems not to be able to assimilate a particular memory trace or samskara and it so obsesses the person that it's good for him or her to get help from a competent therapist or counselor.)

Whenever over a course of time we find ourself unable to progress in meditation or when in an individual meditation session we realize that we are slipping from our position of disinterested observer, we should ask ourself why we are having this difficulty. We will probably find that the answer is fear in some form or other. Perhaps psychologists would use the term "anxiety"; there is a threat to the ego. Even the most elevated observer has an egoic component, and as the ego, at whatever level, begins to feel threatened, it begins to use certain mechanisms to defend itself—at which point we've quit observing and we've started going about our usual way. It's always happening to some extent. Even when we realize we're observing more than we ever have before, we aren't observing as much as we're capable of. What is holding us back is the ego's defensiveness or anxiety or fear. The ego always wants to maintain its integrity. So there's always some degree of ego defense in operation. But when we see that we're not observing as much as we had been, then we should be able to boost ourself back up to the position we had been occupying.

There are various ways, various techniques we can use, to bolster the ego and make it feel more secure so that it can observe more clearly without using ego defense mechanisms. The mechanisms whereby the ego protects itself are basically nonproductive. For example, psychological projection is an extremely common and really quite insane ego defense mechanism. In projection, when something comes up from the unconscious that causes anxiety to the ego, we externalize what we can't accept. We attribute our own thoughts, feelings, or attitudes to others: "My friend is too critical . . . My boss is lazy . . . My parents don't accept me . . . My husband doesn't respect me." We project the thing from the unconscious to someone else and believe that the other person—and not us—is saying it or thinking it or feeling it.

That is one of the cruder and more psychotic defense mechanisms and is very widely used—so widely used that it's almost the way the world runs. We do it in daily life during waking hours, and we can also do it when we're sitting for meditation. Such ego-protective mechanisms are inimical to personal growth. These are ways that perpetuate the ego's narrowness, and even make it more narrow, rigid, and petty. There are, however, other ways that the ego can be made to feel more secure. We can establish certain conditions that serve to allay or even prevent egoic anxiety. For example, part of our ego's defensiveness is always fear of exposure—fear of criticism, ridicule, or censure. Part of our tenacious hold on our ego is due to how we've been relating to other people: what we expect from them, and what we believe they expect from us. One way we can deal with this is to create a situation in which it's not an issue.

We can, for instance, get a therapist who is not judgmental and who is tolerant of letting our ego sort of loosen up. Another thing we can do is to go in an unoccupied room and close the door. Then we're all by ourselves, and whatever we say or do, nobody can hear or see us. Under these conditions our ego can feel safe enough to loosen up a little bit. Many of us do this a lot. In fact, we've gotten to the point that we feel we each have to have a cubicle somewhere that we can go to, because our egos are so oppressive to us and we don't know any other techniques. So often people say, "My privacy is very important," meaning, "I don't know any other way except going in a room and shutting a door to get away from the exhausting necessity of having to play at being this particular person all the time."

Another way to gain respite from our self-created onerous expectations is to cut off our motor involvement with the world. We can voluntarily create a state within ourselves wherein we cannot act, in which we are essentially paralyzed, just as though we'd been given suxnil chloride or curare. When people are given shock treatment, they are first given such an agent to make them paralyzed, so that they can't have violent convulsions and hurt themselves. We can do the same thing voluntarily, without having to take a drug that paralyzes our muscles. We can create a situation in which all our muscles are relaxed and we are in a meditative posture from which we know we are not going to move for a significant length of time. In a manner of speaking, our body is out of gear. If we practice we can get ourselves into such a relaxed state that we know through experience that we're going to stay there for, say, fifteen minutes or a half hour, and that it would really take an act of Congress to get us to move before that time has elapsed. (There are also other techniques we can use to get the body out of gear; Freud used a couch.)

Having cut off our motor involvement with the world, we can now tolerate things coming up that we would never let come up in another situation. We can, for instance, let a feeling of tremendous violent anger come up. We wouldn't let it come up if we were sitting next to the person at whom we've directed all that anger, or if we were busily active, because we're afraid that we might do something. But now there's no one there and there's no tendency toward action, there's complete lack of connection with our motor faculties. So it comes up and we know we're safe; it's safe to let it come up. We're not going to impulsively do something violent; we're not going to impulsively say something that would jeopardize our position in the world or shatter our ego identity. Our voice and our body are out of gear and we're just sitting quietly doing nothing.

There are further conditions that we can create to make the ego more secure so that the process of observation is promoted, facilitated, and we can thus learn and expand and grow. These conditions have to do with delving into the whole question of what anxiety is. Anxiety is that state in which the ego feels that its existence is threatened. But what does it include, what are the concomitants of anxiety? The physiological components of the anxiety state are irregular breathing, muscle tension, rapid heart rate, sweating, and other such responses.

We can utilize techniques—such as breath regulation or posture modification—to change the entire autonomic tone and undercut the development of those autonomic, physiological concomitants of anxiety. These are learnable ways of artificially dissolving the anxiety state, even preventing the anxiety state from occurring. If the anxiety state is undermined that way and cannot come into being, then the ego feels protected, it feels serene. The observer can then sit quietly and watch and not feel threatened. The process of observing and assimilating can therefore proceed much faster.

Another extremely important technique whereby we can establish conditions that make the observer more strong and secure involves the use of the mantra. In the case of the mantra we're doing something more positive than merely eliminating the possibility of anxiety. We are establishing a direction for the observer. We are establishing a sense within ourself of how to relocate the observer in a higher and higher position of observation, a higher and more encompassing perspective. As we said before, as we progress in meditation the observer with which we identify ourselves is going to have to give way to another observer, which is going to have to give way to another observer, and so on. Where are those future observers going to be and how do we get a handle on them? How do we situate that part of our mind in a position that is going to observe more effectively, more comprehensively?

The process can be described as having the observer, while watching the mind, take a step backwards into the unknown, into the unconscious. To feel secure enough to take that step, we need some sense of direction, something that will guide us, something that will give us a sense of the directional course to take. That's where the mantra becomes important. The mantra is a technique that, when properly used, gives us a sense of the direction in which we want to move in reestablishing our position of observation. Without such guidance, we would be fearful that in stepping backwards into the unconscious we would be liable to fall off a ledge right down into all those samskaras that are going to eat us up.

There are a number of possible ways to explain how the mantra works in this manner. But basically the mantra is a sound, and in order to assimilate that sound we have to start by putting that sound into the mind. That means that someone who we consider a competent mantra transmitter tells us that this is the mantra that we should use, and we then begin saying the mantra. That's a first step. We imagine hearing the mantra; we repeat it in our mind. We're not saying it out loud, but we are saying it mentally. In that way the mantra, just like any other thing that we imagine or fantasize, is put into the unconscious. It goes down into the unconscious, and whatever goes in has to come out sooner or later, and the more it goes in, the more it comes out.

How much the mantra goes in depends, of course, not only on how much time but also how much attention and energy we give it. If we simply mechanically say our mantra without paying any real attention while we're also doing something else, it's not going to be there in any substantial way. If, however, we're saying it with feeling and attention and focus and energy, then it goes down and becomes something important in our unconscious. Everything in the subconscious that has any importance or weight to it was put in charged with feeling, emotion, energy, and attention. So we put the mantra in and after some time it begins to come back out. If we quiet the mind, if we really quiet the mind and let the ego dissolve and we stand back and observe as the many samskaras begin to arise, our mantra will be one of them. Then we begin to reach the point where we can be aware of the existence that the mantra has of its own. We can *listen* to the mantra instead of saying the mantra.

If the mantra was correctly prescribed, it's been down in our unconscious all along, but our repetition of it and our salting it away in the subconscious helps us get to the point where we begin to find it in its original formulation. The mantra has always been there; now we're getting in touch with it. It is our listening to the mantra, our attending to it, that helps guide us back to where we need to move—because the mantra is coming from the point where we want to be; the mantra is coming from where we want our consciousness to be centered.

Eventually we reach a stage where we are not so much listening to the mantra as we are being with the mantra. We're listening *from* the mantra, observing *from* the mantra. These, then, are the steps in using the mantra: first we say the mantra, then we listen to the mantra, and eventually we observe from the mantra. In this way it becomes a vitally important guiding technique in the meditative process.

This process of interiorization of the mantra has much to do with subject-object differentiation. When are we the subject and when are we the object? Who or what is the subject and who or what is the object? All of what's going on is inside of us. One part of us is the subject of this action, the other part of us is the object. Gradually we find that the part of us that was the object—that is, the mantra—becomes the subject. The only way to really understand how the mantra operates is to work with it in our own life and experience it ourselves. Only then can we begin to realize, to actually know, what the technique is and what it does.

Mantra is effective in helping us progress more rapidly in self-understanding. But even though mantra gives us some guidance as we step toward more encompassing observer positions, that fact doesn't eliminate the need to observe. We still have to go through all the observing, all the accepting and assimilating; that's a necessary part of the process that can't be bypassed. Meditative observance is a natural growth process. It has two components, which are really just two sides of the same coin: one is our observing, and the other is our positioning ourselves to observe.

Whatever the level of our observance may be, our observing self will not observe what it is not ready to observe. When we sit we need never be afraid that some samskaric monster might be lurking about getting ready to jump up out of our subconscious and devour us. Our witnessing self will see only what it is strong enough to see. As it accepts and assimilates what it sees, it becomes stronger, more expansive, and more secure; its capacity increases, and it can now go to a higher level of observance. This gradualness is a beautiful aspect of meditation. In meditation we never forcibly dredge up things that we aren't ready to deal with; things naturally come up only as and when we create the conditions that are sufficient to tolerate them. There are some therapies that are very confronting; for example, shell-shocked veterans are shown film strips of combat. Certainly this sort of therapy can bring up too much too quickly. Such disturbing and upsetting tactics may not be beneficial at all. Meditation is a gentler and better way.

In meditation, all we really need to do is to not throw roadblocks in the way of the observer. As noted in the beginning, we don't want to have ourselves in such a condition that we're so groggy, overstuffed, or hungry that our attention is preoccupied down on the level of wondering when we are going to get some supper or how we are going to keep our eyes open, so that the observer can't operate. We want to engineer our life in such a way that the observer is not preempted. The observer is preempted by survival issues—food, sleep, sex, self-preservation—instinctual matters that affect the body, that have to be attended to and regulated. If we don't take proper care of these matters, they will preempt our attention, and meditation will not occur. If nothing ever happens to us when we sit for meditation, then we must not be doing a good enough job of attending to our survival issues. That is why we emphasize the necessity of regulating sleep, regulating eating habits, regulating sex.

As for self-preservation: we have to take into consideration the whole question of the ego's fear of annihilation, its basic insecurities. In order for the process of meditation to take place, we have to create a situation in which self-preservation is not a pressing issue. Meditation is basically playful exploring, exploring the unconscious, exploring a vast part of ourselves that we didn't know about before. And the only way that one explores is playfully. Exploration is never done out of desperation or desire for survival; exploration is always done out of curiosity, and because it's exciting, fun, and rewarding. If there's not a sense of playfulness and adventure in the posture and attitude that we have adopted when we sit for meditation, then we may as well not bother with it, for we're not going to get very far.

Children will never play if they feel threatened. That is why children's development is crippled by family situations and social situations in which they feel threatened. They can't grow, they can't explore, they can't learn; they're always defending themselves. The ego is the same way; it's a child. We need to create a situation in which it can feel playful, and then it will progressively explore and learn and expand and grow.

In general, it is most valuable for us to have an active interplay between meditating and being involved in the world. Then, as things come into our awareness in meditation, we have an opportunity to live with the resultant new perspective, to deal with people and situations and ourselves after having assimilated new facets into our personality. This is an ongoing process. Persistent systematic meditation can give us an ever-new way of dealing with the world, of being in the world.

Thus, if we're meditating properly, if we're beginning to learn to carry the fruits of our meditative efforts out into the world for all to share and enjoy, then there should be a sense of each day or at least each week being a new experience. There's a new perspective, there's a new *I* that is dealing with the world, so the world looks different and experiences feel different and we react differently.

This is the aliveness, the joy, that is really the

birthright of every human being. We should sense that. When we don't, we're not living up to our potential. Meditation can definitely help us experience that aliveness and keep us actively involved in a process of growth and ever-increasing self-realization.

The Tradition of
Superconscious Meditation

Pandit Usharbudh Arya, D.Litt.

To understand Superconscious Meditation, one first needs to understand the Superconscious itself. In the system of Superconscious Meditation one does not move from some unconscious principle toward a higher state of experience, but rather, what seems to many as a separate and higher state actually encompasses all degrees of consciousness, even the seemingly unconscious. In fact the prefix *super* is used only for linguistic convenience; otherwise it is redundant. All that is of life and consciousness is of the Superconscious principle. Life is not regarded as a process, nor is consciousness an experience between subject and object; life and consciousness, *jiva* and *chit,* are one and the same; they are two names of an entity, a force, a field of energy. The field of energy, *shakti,* and the one who knows this field, who is conscious of it, are also one and the same. This total unity is Superconsciousness. What is signified by the abstract noun *Superconsciousness,* and by the adjective *Superconscious,* is indivisible. The Superconscious is one being, the name of all names, that from which all subjects, objects, and experiences arise, in which they have their existence and continuity, and into which they finally subside as though never having arisen as separated experiences.

Everything we have said above has been said before by all the saints and yogis. We can only illustrate it somewhat, which we shall attempt to do. But why do it? Simply because what has been said before is not now within the experience of those who view themselves as separate units of consciousness. To understand the Superconscious is to be in that state of meditation in which the primary experience is such unity. Because the system of Superconscious Meditation is a living tradition of those who have lived in this experience as their primary mode of being, it emphasizes not the intellectual philosophy but the experience of this mode of existence as a goal for everyone. Thus, Superconsciousness should not be viewed as one state among many, but as the total mode of existence. Being is consciousness and consciousness is being; *sat* is *chit* and *chit* is *sat*. Most protagonists of meditation speak of going into meditation and coming out of it. This way of using words makes meditation seem to be just one state among many, with a beginning, a process, and an ending. In the Superconscious these modes of becoming, transience, and change do not apply; all that is said is from the vantage point of the indivisible unity.

Let us try to understand this by using the analogy of the ocean. Philosophers often speak of the unity of waves with the ocean. But, again, they are speaking from the beach, from the shore, viewing the waves and just trying to imagine an ocean. However, let us shift from the shore and merge our consciousness with that of the ocean, an ocean aware of itself. Think of the sea becoming aware of itself, its total self, from the Arctic to the Antarctic, from the depths of the Marianas Trench to all the beaches of all the continents and islands of the whole earth. How does this self-aware sea view itself? How does a human being view all parts of his personality or body? Do we not know our nose and our toes all as one self? So, the self-aware sea sees its entire planetary existence, with all the tides, beaches, waves, depths, and bubbles all at once and knows itself to be one.

What a bubble is to the sea, the entire universe—with all its atoms and galaxies and vast space—is to the Superconscious. We are not speaking of the awareness that a bubble, a universe, or an individual human being has of itself in relation to the ocean, the Superconscious, but of the awareness that the sea has of the bubble and of itself, the awareness that the Superconscious Being has of itself and of the bubbles known as the universes, with all their transient spaces, times, and causations. This awareness is Superconscious Meditation.

Superconscious Meditation, thus, is not a transcendental experience. It is not an altered state of consciousness, because it is not a state which can be considered the equal to some other state. The consciousness of a bubble may be compared to that of another bubble or of a wave, but an ocean's awareness of itself is neither an alteration in the bubble's consciousness nor a transcending of it. A human being does not arrive at the conclusion of being one complete whole by first transcending an awareness of his different parts. When one says "I," it includes all dimensions of oneself, all experiences and memories, all expectations, and all that lies hidden as unmanifest and of which the existence as a potential has not yet been suspected. So is the consciousness of one who dwells in Superconscious Meditation. Since there is nothing below or above it, nothing before or beyond in this all-inclusive universe beyond the universe, there is nothing to transcend. All things and thoughts are its emanations.

All other states are its derivatives. The emanations and derivatives are not excluded from it, but merely seen in proper perspective of where they belong.

In other words, all that we experience of the three states of consciousness—what we see in wakefulness, dream, or sleep, whatever we can imagine or create with and without our minds—are simply modes, modifications, and waves arising from the Superconscious. The Superconscious is their substratum. The waves of time, space, and causation in the objective universe and in subjective experience arise on the bosom of this ocean and are included in it. The energy of their birth and momentum, as well as their termination, is derived from and arises from the tranquil depths of this sea, but the depths are unaffected by these phenomena occurring on the surface. The ocean in its awareness knows both the depths and the shallows, and sends forth its energy to them. In such an oceanic consciousness of a realized master, or a *siddha,* there is no "going into" meditation. A master of Superconscious Meditation needs no processes or techniques to go into meditation. It is said in an ancient text: That you go into meditation is your bondage.

For those who have not yet merged their awareness into that of the ocean, there have to be processes and techniques. Of this we will speak a little later. Let us first understand the source of this teaching. The process of the emanation of the manifest from the unmanifest is the process of teaching. Various individual minds are the eddies and whirls in the sea called the Golden Womb. All the energies manifest in these eddies and whirls are energies of the Golden Womb. When waves arise from the sea, the sea itself does not increase, nor is the sea diminished when the waves recede. Such is the nature of the Golden Womb. Even if the whole universe disappears, it merely becomes unmanifest to its own manifoldness; the Golden Womb remains as ever, eternally.

The minds of great *rishis,* saints, and masters are those powerful tides in the Golden Womb that carry along huge and little waves as they move. The conscious energy of the little waves rides on the back of these tides when a group of disciples is led by a guru, the remover of darkness. Little minds are linked to greater minds, which in turn dwell as one in the Golden Womb. There is no other process of teaching meditation. Only those who understand this link and the process of linkage can teach meditation. A bubble cannot teach another bubble; it is taught by a larger wave from which it derives the energy for its very existence, continuity, and dissolution. The sea loves all its bubbles but is itself more than the sum total of them all.

In other words, the true process (if such a term may be used) of Superconscious Meditation depends not so much on an individual's trying to enter into meditation—going in from outside—but on his being pulled within. It is not that the disciple increases his capacity but that more and more energy is poured into him. As one master has said: The guru pushes from without and pulls from within. It is not so much a matter of an individual's ascent as of his being elevated. On the part of the individuated wave of awareness, called a person, it is not a filling of oneself that constitutes meditation but an emptying of oneself of all phenomenal experience and its residue, so that the tides of the Golden Womb may take over.

This amazing wonder of the waves of bliss and the waves of beauty is celebrated and sung of in *Saundarya-*

lahari (*Song of the Waves of Beauty*), one of the two major texts of Superconscious Meditation, composed by the great Shankaracharya. One initiated into the secrets of this great text is called *Shriman* in India, that is, one endowed with *shri,* the energy of total life and consciousness. According to the second verse of *Saundarya-lahari,* the Creator takes a molecule of the dust from the feet of the goddess Shri and flings it wide; that one molecule of dust from Her feet is the whole universe. What She herself is can be known only to those who, in the words of the *Bhagavad Gita,* have seen the light of a thousand suns shining simultaneously in the sky.

The other important text of the system of Superconscious Meditation is the *Mandukya Karika,* the expository verses of the sage Gaudapada on the *Mandukya Upanishad.* The *Mandukya Upanishad* is one of the shortest Upanishads, expounding the mysteries of the word OM in twelve sentences. Gaudapada wrote 234 verses of exposition on this Upanishad. Shankaracharya—who was the disciple of Govindapada, who was Gaudapada's disciple—wrote a detailed commentary on this work, and other commentators have followed in his footsteps. Like *Saundarya-lahari,* the *karikas* also can be understood fully only by one who dwells in Superconsciousness. We can speak only as a bubble would, and not as one with the oceanic consciousness.

Superconsciousness is described in the seventh verse of the *Mandukya Upanishad* in these words:

> Not inwardly cognitive, nor outwardly cognitive, nor cognitive both ways, nor a cognition-mass; neither cognitive, nor non-cognitive. Unseen, non-empirical, not apprehended, without

marks (indefinable), inconceivable, indescribable; as the essence of one-self awareness, the cessation of the warp (of phenomena); pacific, benevolent, and non-dual. They meditate on this fourth. That is to be known as the Self.

This description is given only after defining, not denying, the other three states of consciousness. One of Gaudapada's thrusts is in the direction of comparing the realities witnessed in the three states. All states of consciousness are internally self-evident. No external evidence can be found to prove or disprove the accuracy of the experience of any state of consciousness. The laws that apply to one state do not apply to another. An upright object in a box may fall when the box is tilted, but a castle in one's head remains upright even when the head is tilted in wakefulness, in a daydream, or in a dream. The experiences of the wakeful state end when one falls asleep and begins to dream; the experiences of the dream state end with wakefulness. In the dream state the phenomena of the wakeful world are not valid, and so also the dream world is unreal while one is awake. The two levels of reality negate each other.

All experiences last only as long as the thoughts of them last. That alone is their duration. Whatever permanence can be attributed to them is dependent only on the duration of the thought of permanence, and no more. The entire universe, then, is a long-lasting dream of the universal soul. Just as the individual wave has its true awakening into meditation, so also the universal soul realizes its true being only when it knows that the Superconscious reality alone is its origin. Then the universal soul, too, is liberated from the warp of phenomena. The universal mind then returns to its own origins beyond.

We have spoken so far only of consciousness as it is experienced by an accomplished one, an adept, a *siddha,* or a master. What about the rest of us, who are yet bubbles very proud of the little colors reflecting in us, aware only of the three seconds of our life span, not knowing most of the time even that a universe exists, let alone the grand Deity? Indeed, for us, the prefix *super* in the word Superconscious is not redundant. Meditation for us is a process, an upward climb, or a downward dive. To understand Superconscious Meditation in terms of an individual, *pinda,* it is necessary to understand the entire process of the unfoldment of a universe from within consciousness. The dictum "Whatever is in the person is in the universe" has a far-reaching significance. The return of the individual consciousness to the great oceanic Superconsciousness takes place through a long journey consisting of the gradual opening of many gates, one after another. What seems to be an opening from one end is a closing when seen from another side. This again can be understood only when the process of creation of the thought called the universe is grasped, at least intellectually.

Creation is a negative process. It takes place only through the selection of a few of the potentials, or *shaktis,* of the Omnipotent. For example, only a few of these *shaktis* are responsible for the fact that water is cool or for the ability of statesmen to make statements. In a given entity or personality the rest of the *shaktis* are asleep, denied an awakening, and *not* selected for unfoldment. So, one examining a bubble can scarcely grasp the meaning of a whole tidal force. As consciousness expands in meditation, more and more of what seemed dormant comes awake, is re-cognized (*pratyabhijna*). A wave has more *shaktis* than a bubble has.

The tradition of Superconscious Meditation has attempted to list some of the major unfoldments that take place as the Superconscious becomes the universe in a small part of its consciousness. This process is called creation, *shrishti.* The opposite process of the merger of each category back into its respective origin, in the reverse order, is called withdrawal, *samhara,* dissolution. Let us here examine the two processes further. The universe we know is a thought in the Superconscious Principle. When the thought is withdrawn, the universe ceases to be. When a specific thought is withdrawn, it merges into a more encompassing thought from which it arose; the given thought thus ceases to be, and merges into the unmanifest. These thoughts are the objects, entities, and personalities, the species and genera; parts and whole; time, space, causation, and their coordinates; the subjects, objects, and experiences; the entire set of universal processes and laws; the entire set called the universe. This is the entire process of creation and dissolution.

Now, in the individuated awareness of a person the same process occurs as thoughts arise and vanish. When the force of a given thought gives way to a higher awareness from which the various parts of individual thoughts had arisen, it becomes a meditative experience. Thus, the process of the creation and dissolution of an individual's thoughts concerning the universe or its specific objects, entities, and so forth directly corresponds to the processes of creation and dissolution of the whole universe—which is, again, an entire thought of the Superconscious.

So we need to examine the categories into which the thoughts of the Superconscious—as they arise in creation and are withdrawn in dissolution of the universe—appear and disappear. The individual thoughts of a person are thoughts about these universal thoughts and are not otherwise original. As the objects and entities of the universe become manifold from one, so the minds that think of them also have become manifold from one mind. The two are, in fact, inseparable. An object lasts in experience only as long as the thought of it lasts. According to the tradition of Superconscious Meditation, the categories of these thoughts in creation are as follows, in the order of manifestation. The order of dissolution of the universe, which is the same as the order of an individual's meditative expansion and liberation from the confinement of limiting thoughts, is the reverse.

Here, then, is the unfoldment, the narrowing down, of *shaktis* into the objective universe: (1) *Shiva,* Superconsciousness, ever-pure, ever-wise, ever-free; (2) *Maheshvara,* the great Lord, imbued with the power of activity (*rajas*), creator of the universe, the creative power; (3) *sadashiva,* supporter, cause of the continuity of the universe, the supporting power; (4) the power to dissolve, *kāla-shakti,* the power of time; (5) *shuddha-vidya,* pure knowledge, the liberating force; (6) *maya,* the limiting knowledge; (7) *kāla,* time; (8a) *niyati,* the power to control and direct toward a goal or destiny; (8b) *kalā,* the three hundred and sixty degrees of all objects and experiences, aspects; (9) *vidya,* the knowledge of specific alternatives (limited); (10) *raga,* attraction and desire; (11) *purusha,* the individuated consciousness principle, the soul; (12) *prakriti,* the original nature or matter maintaining an inner balance of the three *gunas;* (13) the three *gunas: sattva,* harmony; *rajas,* activity; *tamas,* stasis; (14) *buddhi,* discriminatory knowledge, whereby the individuated person may know itself to be separate from objective, material identifications; (15) *ahankara,* the ego, both universal and personal; (16) *manas,* the power to meditate; (17) the five *pranas: prana, apana, vyana, udana,* and *samana;* (18) the seven physiological components: skin, blood, flesh, fat, bone, marrow, and sexual fluids; (19) the active senses: speech, the hands, the feet, and the organs of elimination and of generation; (20) the cognitive senses: the ears, the skin (for touch), the eyes, the tongue (for taste), and the nose (for smell); (21) the five *tan-matras,* the five principles of the elements: sound, sight, tactility, flavor, and odor; from these the five gross elements are created; (22) the five states of matter, the grosser ones arising from the finer, starting with space, then gases, fire, liquid (water), and finally solid (earth).

In a different and more concise way of listing, these are the total of twenty-five stages of the unfoldment: *sadashiva, maheshvara, shuddha-vidya, maya, manas,* the five *tan-matras,* and the five states of matter. All of these have been translated and included in the previous listing. All that there is in the universe is a modification of these, and there are no thoughts but thoughts of these in all of the possible combinations and permutations. Sound, for example, combined with other energies becomes the alphabet, which becomes language for communication and mantra and meditation. The understanding of the energies of all of the possible letters of the alphabet and the way they interact with the powers of other thoughts are all taught in the tradition of Superconscious Meditation.

When the words *higher* and *lower* are used in metaphysical language they refer to the relationships among these various energies of negation and unfoldment. The number twenty-two in the list is lower than the number twenty-one, and so on back to number one. The lowest meditation is at the level of number twenty-two. A beginner starts at this point, the five states of matter, transcends it, and goes on to a higher experience. Or he may start (with the advice of a teacher) at any point that comes naturally to him, at the level of awareness that he has developed. Here two different processes occur.

One—the most important process—is of *shaktipata,* the descent of energies. As the bubble moves toward a wave, the wave engulfs it and imparts to it its own expanded nature and force of awareness. A higher teacher uplifts the lower student. The less powerful charge of energy is picked up by the more powerful. The consciousness contracts from its previous horizon and expands into the greater horizon. The identification changes from the lower to the higher, from the grosser to the finer. It becomes more encompassing, less negating.

The total capacity, the total energy level, of the individual rises and expands. Think of this by using the analogy of the life function of a person very near to death as compared with an athlete participating in an Olympic race. There is a vast difference between the two. There are also only very fine degrees of difference between the two. This is the difference between the capacity of a master and a student; one wills, the other wishes. One creates a whole universe as mere thought, with mere thought. The other separates the thought from the thing, and this prevents him from exercising total mastery over the thing, or over the situation. As the higher energies are infused into the lower, the lower consciousness rises and overcomes all obstacles in the meditative path, both of psychic and of objective nature. Like a flood, the flow of energy tears down all barriers in the path of meditation.

This expansion is just another side of a contraction. All objects and thoughts arise from a fine point, *bindu.* The power of a nuclear bomb—expanding to cover an entire city or more—is centered in a point, bindu, of the nucleus. It is by realizing the power of that invisible bindu that the nuclear fission or fusion is accomplished. So each unfolded object in the universe, and each thought, has a bindu, a point of origin and dissolution. The consciousness expands—that is, it contracts into the bindu. When one first masters the principles of solid matter through meditation, it is as if the limited consciousness knocks against an invisible point in the wall of energy in the mind. Suddenly the point bursts, opening a gateway to the next higher energy; an initiation has occurred. So it goes on; no matter what object, what thought, what chakra or mantra is used for meditation, this bursting through an indefinable point has to take place.

In that process of bursting through all three hundred and sixty degrees of time and space, all the triangles of the object or thought are transcended, overpowered, and made into the tools of one's own will. The energy of the lower consciousness is pulled into that of the higher. The higher includes the lower, but the lower does not include the higher. Thoughts include objects, but objects do not include thoughts. There is not the slightest difference between the processes of *shaktipata* and *bindu-bhedana,* the descent of energy and the fission of a point. Contraction is expansion; a flight is a dive; opening a door is closing the same.

In *Saundarya-lahari* these processes are described in step-by-step detail. The realized masters tell us that each of the hundred verses in *Song of the Waves of Beauty* contains a thousand meditative accomplishments, to be understood by individuals only through their personal experience. Gaudapada, following the system of the *Mandukya Upanishad,* has reduced the entire universe and the meditative process to three points and then to the pointless, the final expansion. We have spoken so far in terms of grace flowing from a higher source to a lower. This is known as *shrishti-matrika,* the creative process. Techniques alone cannot reach there; the technique is itself only *samhara-matrika,* the process of withdrawal, or the preparation for grace.

Superconscious Meditation is a complete philosophy and system because it deals with *each* of the elements and thoughts of each category of the universe, and offers both a technique and an unfoldment of energy through grace at each level.

Appendix A:
Breathing Exercises

The following exercises will assist one in developing the practice of meditation. Students interested in learning further about meditation are also encouraged to continue their study with several other Institute publications: *Lectures on Yoga* by Swami Rama, *Yoga Psychology* by Swami Ajaya, and *Mantra and Meditation* by Dr. Usharbudh Arya.

Simple Deep-Breathing Exercise

One simple deep-breathing exercise is to lie on the back with the feet a comfortable distance apart and the arms along the sides of the body, palms up. Gently close the eyes and place the hands on the upper abdomen, between the rib cage and the navel, in order to feel the movement of the muscles. Inhale and exhale through the nostrils slowly, smoothly, and deeply. There should be no noise, jerks, or pauses in the breath. Exaggerating the normal breathing process, consciously pull in the abdominal muscles while exhaling. Aspirants who find difficulty in practicing this diaphragmatic movement may use their hands to gently push in the abdominal muscles when exhaling. When inhaling be aware of the abdominal

Sections of this appendix are excerpted from the book *Lectures on Yoga*, by Swami Rama, published by the Himalayan Institute.

wall pushing out. There should be a slight movement of the chest. Practice this method of deep breathing three to five minutes a day until you clearly understand the movement of the diaphragm.

Relaxation with Breathing

Relaxation with breathing has been proven useful for nervousness and other diseases. Lie down on your back with a soft pillow under your head. Begin exhaling and inhaling slowly and deeply, breathing diaphragmatically. First, relax your limbs physically, and then ask your mind to travel, with a feeling of relaxation, toward your toes. Do this systematically, centering on each set of muscles throughout the body and relaxing them. Start by relaxing your forehead, the facial muscles, neck, shoulders, and so on, continuing down until you reach the toes. Then return back to the head, relaxing each set of muscles along the way. Do not allow any other feelings to intrude during this exercise.

After relaxing for five minutes, you can create voluntary tension all over the body and try to maintain the state of tension for at least sixty seconds. Then gradually relax all parts of the body again, systematically, from head to toes. Relax, create voluntary tension, then relax again, exhaling and inhaling slowly and deeply. If you concentrate on the deep and even flow of breath and form the habit of deep inhalation and exhalation, you will find that you can easily relax. In cases of fatigue, deep-breathing with relaxation has been proven to be very beneficial, but retention of the breath should be avoided. You can even relax at your office desk for five minutes, refresh yourself, and thus increase immensely your capacity for doing work.

Nadi Shodhana—Channel Purification

This is a breathing exercise which purifes the *nadis*, or subtle energy channels. It should be done at least twice a day—in the morning and in the evening. In the morning nadi shodhana is done in the following manner:

1. Sit in a calm, quiet, airy place in an easy and steady posture.

2. Keep the head, neck and trunk straight and the body still.

3. Bring the right hand up to the nose. The index finger and middle finger should be folded so that the right thumb can be used to close the right nostril and the ring finger can be used to close the left nostril.

4. Close the right nostril with the right thumb. Exhale completely through the left nostril. The exhalation should be slow, controlled, and free from exertion and jerks.

5. At the end of the exhalation close the left nostril with the ring finger, open the right nostril, and inhale slowly and completely. Inhalation and exhalation should be of equal duration.

6. Repeat this cycle of exhalation with the left nostril and inhalation with the right nostril two more times.

7. At the end of the third inhalation through the right nostril, exhale completely through the same nostril, still keeping the left nostril closed with the ring finger.

8. At the end of the exhalation, close the right nostril with the thumb and inhale through the left nostril.

9. Repeat the cycle of exhalation through the right nostril and inhalation through the left nostril two more times. This completes the exercise.

To sum up, the exercise consists of:

(a) Three cycles of exhalation through the left nostril and inhalation through the right nostril followed by

(b) Three cycles of exhalation through the right nostril and inhalation through the left nostril.

In the evening the exercise consists of:

(a) Three cycles of exhalation through the right nostril and inhalation through the left nostril followed by

(b) Three cycles of exhalation through the left nostril and inhalation through the right nostril.

Be careful to see that inhalation and exhalation are of equal duration and are slow, controlled, and free from jerks as well as any sense of exertion. With time, gradual lengthening of the duration of inhalation and exhalation should be attempted.

There are many other types of *pranayama,* each having a specific purpose, and some of these will now be described briefly.

Kapalabhati Pranayama

In literal translation *kapalabhati* means "the *pranayama* which makes the skull shine." It is practiced in a stable posture with the head, neck, and trunk erect and in one line. The exercise consists of a vigorous, forceful expulsion of breath, using the diaphragm and abdominal muscles, followed by a relaxation of the abdominal muscles resulting in a spontaneous inhalation. This constitutes one cycle. Several cycles are repeated in quick succession. In the beginning one attempts between seven and twenty-one cycles, depending on one's capacity. This exercise cleans the sinuses and respiratory passages and stimulates the abdominal muscles and digestive organs.

Bhastrika Pranayama

Bhastra means bellows, and in this exercise the abdominal muscles move forcefully in and out like a blacksmith's bellows. In this *pranayama* both exhalation and inhalation are vigorous and forceful. Together, they constitute one cycle, and several cycles (between seven and twenty-one) are to be repeated in quick succession. There are three variations of *bhastrika*—front bellows, side-to-side bellows, and alternate bellows. The front bellows is done in the same position as kapalabhati.

In the side-to-side bellows the first burst of exhalation and inhalation is made with the head facing front. Now turn the head fully to the right (in the morning, but to the left in the evening) and repeat the rapid exhalation and inhalation. Now the head is turned back to the front and the exhalation-inhalation is repeated. Then to the left — exhale and inhale with a burst—and back to the front. This is one cycle. It may be repeated between seven and twenty-one times.

In the alternate bellows the rapid exhalation-inhalation is done with one nostril at a time. The thumb of the right hand is used to close the right nostril and the rapid exhalation-inhalation takes place through the left nostril. Then the left nostril is closed with the middle or ring finger of the right hand, and the rapid exhalation-inhalation takes place through the right nostril. This sequence of left nostril exhalation-inhalation and then right nostril exhalation-inhalation applies to the morning practice. It is reversed (right nostril first and then left nostril) in the evening. The exhalation and inhalation should be vigorous and forceful, using the abdominal muscles and diaphragm, not the chest. The cycle may be repeated about twenty-one times. The benefits of the *bhastrika pranayama* are similar to those of *kapalabhati pranayama:* the forceful exhalation cleans the lungs of the stale residual air which is not removed in normal breathing, the entire respiratory system is purified, and internal vigor is aroused.

Rhythmic breathing, breathing with relaxation, and the *nadi shodhana* (channel purification) may be practiced by the beginner. Then, but only after some practice, the *kapalabhati* and *bhastrika pranayamas* may be attempted.

Appendix B:
Beginning the Practice of Meditation

Optimum preliminaries to the practice of meditation include an undisturbed emotional life, created by the practice of a loving ethical code, and an undistracted mental life, created by skillfully scheduling and completing one's tasks. In this way, one aims to avoid disturbing either oneself or others. A healthy and comfortable physical environment, promoted by regulation of one's bodily needs, including proper diet and exercise, also aids in the practice of meditation, for it keeps one free from pain and fatigue.

When sitting for meditation, one should select a clean, quiet, and secluded place and a time free from interruption. These should be kept constant in order to elicit a meditation response, and this will prepare the mind and body for regular daily practice. After rising and before retiring are excellent times, and twilight is also good. Meditation is easier when practiced with the stomach, bowels, and bladder empty. Wearing loose comfortable clothing and cleansing the body make one feel fresh for meditation. The nasal wash is an excellent preparatory exerise. (For a description of the nasal wash, see *Lectures on Yoga*.)

Having selected a time and place for meditation, a meditative posture suited to one's own physical makeup should be selected and practiced regularly. Sitting on the edge of a straightback chair in the friendship pose or on the floor in variations of the easy, auspicious, or accomplished poses is advised. A firm cushion of appropriate height may be wedged behind the buttocks to tilt the hips properly, thereby relieving back discomfort. Cushions placed under the knees provide better support, however.

The practice of meditation is best preceded by a series of easy stretches and a period of relaxation in which one surveys the entire body from head to toe and back again, releasing all areas of tension as one goes. Breathing practices are done in a sitting position, including the bellows breath, alternate nostril breathing, and diaphragmatic breathing. One's posture should be straight with the head, neck, and trunk aligned, and the pose should be comfortable and steady. Upon assuming a sitting pose, one should remain as still and relaxed as possible for the duration of one's practice time. One can begin with periods of five to ten minutes and, as one's capacity gradually expands, extend it to twenty to thirty minutes or more.

A period of breath awareness is the next step. The breathing should be made smooth and deep without any pauses or sounds. Observing the flow of breath through the nostrils will help concentrate the mind and regulate the breathing. Focusing on the point where the upper lip meets the bridge between the nostrils will help equalize the flow of air through both nostrils, thereby leading to a tranquil state of mind more conducive to meditation.

Having drawn one's attention inward to the here and now, one is ready to apply one's concentration to a sound vibration, or *mantra*. The universal mantra *so hum* can be used beneficially by those who have not been given a personal mantra by a qualified teacher from an established tradition. One should remember the sound "so" upon inhalation and the sound "hum" upon exhalation. This mantra means "I am That," and it helps one to realize one's true nature. The word "That" refers to the divine inner dweller who is one's true Self.

When distractions in the form of thoughts, images, emotions, sensations, or external stimuli occur, one simply allows them to flow by and keeps the mind focused on the mantra, with the breathing regular and the posture straight. One does not judge, edit, analyze, embellish, critique, or in any way react to one's inner experiencing. One simply observes, as a neutral objective witness, whatever passes by, and when the mind wanders, one simply brings it back to the focus of concentration.

Having stilled the body, the breath, and the conscious mind, the unconscious mind becomes more active. By maintaining a state of mental and physical calmness through posture, breath, and concentration, emotional upset due to this unconscious material does not occur. Autonomic arousal and perturbing self-talks are limited by meditative interventions, and with practice, one desensitizes oneself to potentially noxious or tempting material and gains greater self-understanding and emotional control. Remaining tranquil in the face of adversity then becomes a useful skill that one carries over into daily life.

In the process of practicing meditation regularly, one learns constant, ardent, and conscious focusing of the mind and emotions on the mantra, which is a positive and uplifting thought form. One then becomes tacitly aware of a deeper level of one's being. Thus one has more direct experience of one's higher Self. This results in the eventual formulation of a personal philosophy of life based on the direct experience of a reality beyond and within the everyday physical world. The voice of one's conscience then becomes clearer and serves as an inner teacher to guide and inspire one. Greater meaning and purpose in life, resulting in increased spiritual fulfillment and peace, are then attained.

About the Authors

 **Swami Rama** is founder and spiritual head of the Himalayan International Institute of Yoga Science and Philosophy. Raised in the cave monasteries of the Himalayas, he has also been formally educated in some of the most prestigious universities of both the East and West and has served as consultant to research centers such as the Menninger Foundation. He is the author of *Living with the Himalayan Masters, A Practical Guide to Holistic Health, Lectures on Yoga,* and numerous other books.

 **Swami Ajaya, Ph.D.,** has practiced clinical psychology for the past eighteen years and has acted as a consultant to several mental health centers. He was educated at Wesleyan University and the University of California at Berkeley. After serving as a postdoctoral fellow at the University of Wisconsin Department of Psychiatry and teaching at the University, he traveled and studied with various sages of India, being ordained a monk by Swami Rama. Swami Ajaya is the author of *Psychotherapy East and West: A Unifying Paradigm* and *Yoga Psychology,* the coauthor of *Yoga and Psychotherapy,* and the editor of several other books.

Arpita, Ph.D., is on the faculty of the Himalayan Institute. Formerly, she served as assistant director of psychological services at the Institute of Rehabilitation Medicine of Allied Services, Inc. She received her doctorate in counselor education with a specialty in counseling psychology from Pennsylvania State University. Her research has included the investigation of the effects of diaphragmatic breathing and hatha yoga. Dr. Arpita is the author of *Yoga Psychology and the Beatitudes* and has assisted in the production of several other books.

Pandit Usharbudh Arya, D.Litt., is founder and director of the Center for Higher Consciousness. Born in the priestly tradition of the Brahmins of India, Dr. Arya holds a Master of Arts degree from the University of London and a Doctor of Literature degree from the University of Utrecht. He is a former professor of Sanskrit and Indian religions at the University of Minnesota and a recipient of its Distinguished Teacher's Award. Among the books he has written are *Mantra and Meditation, Meditation and the Art of Dying, God, Superconscious Meditation,* and *Philosophy of Hatha Yoga.*

Rudolph Ballentine, M.D., is president of the Himalayan International Institute of the U.S.A. After receiving his M.D. from Duke University, he studied psychology at the University of Paris (Sorbonne) and was subsequently appointed assistant clinical professor of psychiatry at Louisiana State University, New Orleans. He is presently director of the Combined Therapy Program of the Himalayan Institute. He lectures extensively around the country and has written *Diet and Nutrition: A Holistic Approach* and coauthored *Yoga and Psychotherapy* as well as *Science of Breath: A Practical Guide.*

Phil Nuernberger, Ph.D., author of *Freedom from Stress: A Holistic Approach,* is on the faculty of the Himalayan Institute, where he is particularly involved in the Stress Management Program. He received his Ph.D. in psychology from the University of Minnesota. He is a former director of biofeedback therapy at a major neurological and psychiatric clinic in the Midwest. Dr. Nuernberger serves as a consultant to several large corporations and is a contributing author to *Theory and Practice of Meditation, Psychology East and West,* and *Meditational Therapy.*

The main building of the national headquarters, Honesdale, Pa.

The Himalayan Institute

The Himalayan International Institute of Yoga Science and Philosophy of the U.S.A. is a nonprofit organization devoted to the scientific and spiritual progress of modern humanity. Founded in 1971 by Sri Swami Rama, the Institute combines Western and Eastern teachings and techniques to develop educational, therapeutic, and research programs for serving people in today's world. The goals of the Institute are to teach meditational techniques for the growth of individuals and their society, to make known the harmonious view of world religions and philosophies, and to undertake scientific research for the benefit of humankind.

This challenging task is met by people of all ages, all walks of life, and all faiths who attend and participate in the Institute courses and seminars. These programs, which are given on a continuing basis, are designed in order that one may discover for oneself how to live more creatively. In the words of Swami Rama, "By being aware of one's own potential and abilities, one can become a perfect citizen, help the nation, and serve humanity."

The Institute has branch centers and affiliates throughout the United States. The 422-acre campus of the national headquarters, located in the Pocono Mountains of northeastern Pennsylvania, serves as the coordination center for all the Institute activities, which include a wide variety of innovative programs in education, research, and therapy, combining Eastern and Western approaches to self-awareness and self-directed change.

SEMINARS, LECTURES, WORKSHOPS, and CLASSES are available throughout the year, providing intensive training and experience in such topics as Superconscious Meditation, hatha yoga, philosophy, psychology, and various aspects of personal growth and holistic health. The *Himalayan News,* a free bimonthly publication, announces the current programs.

The RESIDENTIAL and SELF-TRANSFORMATION PROGRAMS provide training in the basic yoga disciplines— diet, ethical behavior, hatha yoga, and meditation. Students are also given guidance in a philosophy of living in a community environment.

The PROGRAM IN EASTERN STUDIES AND COMPARATIVE PSYCHOLOGY offers a unique and systematic synthesis of Western empirical sources and Eastern introspective science. Masters and Doctoral-level studies may be pursued through cross-registration with several accredited colleges and universities.

The five-day STRESS MANAGEMENT PROGRAM offers practical and individualized training that can be used to control the stress response. This includes biofeedback, relaxation skills, exercise, diet, breathing techniques, and meditation.

A yearly INTERNATIONAL CONGRESS, sponsored by the Institute, is devoted to the scientific and spiritual progress of modern humanity. Through lectures, workshops, seminars, and practical demonstrations, it provides a forum for professionals and lay people to share their knowledge and research.

The ELEANOR N. DANA RESEARCH LABORATORY is the psychophysiological laboratory of the Institute, specializing in research on breathing, meditation, holistic therapies, and stress and relaxed states. The laboratory is fully equipped for exercise stress testing and psychophysiological measurements, including brain waves, patterns of respiration, heart rate changes, and muscle tension. The staff investigates Eastern teachings through studies based on Western experimental techniques.

Himalayan Institute Publications

Living with the Himalayan Masters   Swami Rama
Lectures on Yoga   Swami Rama
A Practical Guide to Holistic Health   Swami Rama
Choosing a Path   Swami Rama
Inspired Thoughts of Swami Rama   Swami Rama
Freedom from the Bondage of Karma   Swami Rama
Book of Wisdom (Ishopanishad)   Swami Rama
Enlightenment Without God   Swami Rama
Exercise Without Movement   Swami Rama
Life Here and Hereafter   Swami Rama
Marriage, Parenthood, and Enlightenment   Swami Rama
Path of Fire and Light   Swami Rama
Perennial Psychology of the Bhagavad Gita   Swami Rama
Love Whispers   Swami Rama
Creative Use of Emotion   Swami Rama, Swami Ajaya
Science of Breath   Swami Rama, Rudolph Ballentine, M.D., Alan Hymes, M.D.
Yoga and Psychotherapy   Swami Rama, Rudolph Ballentine, M.D., Swami Ajaya
Superconscious Meditation   Usharbudh Arya, D.Litt.
Mantra and Meditation   Usharbudh Arya, D.Litt.
Philosophy of Hatha Yoga   Usharbudh Arya, D.Litt.
Meditation and the Art of Dying   Usharbudh Arya, D.Litt.
God   Usharbudh Arya, D.Litt.
Yoga sutras of Patanjali, Volume I   Usharbudh Arya, D.Litt.
Psychotherapy East and West: A Unifying Paradigm   Swami Ajaya, Ph.D.
Yoga Psychology   Swami Ajaya, Ph.D.
Psychology East and West   Swami Ajaya, Ph.D. (ed.)
Meditational Therapy   Swami Ajaya, Ph.D. (ed.)
Diet and Nutrition   Rudolph Ballentine, M.D.
Joints and Glands Exercises   Rudolph Ballentine, M.D. (ed.)

Theory and Practice of Meditation	Rudolph Ballentine, M.D. (ed.)
Freedom from Stress	Phil Nuernberger, Ph.D.
Science Studies Yoga	James Funderburk, Ph.D.
Homeopathic Remedies	Drs. Anderson, Buegel, Chernin
Hatha Yoga Manual I	Samskrti and Veda
Hatha Yoga Manual II	Samskrti and Judith Franks
Seven Systems of Indian Philosophy	R. Tigunait, Ph.D.
Swami Rama of the Himalayas	L. K. Misra, Ph.D. (ed.)
Philosophy of Death and Dying	M. V. Kamath
Practical Vedanta of Swami Rama Tirtha	Brandt Dayton (ed.)
The Swami and Sam	Brandt Dayton
Yoga Psychology and the Beatitudes	S. Arpita, Ph.D.
Yoga and Christianity	Justin O'Brien, D.Th.
Himalayan Mountain Cookery	Martha Ballentine
The Yoga Way Cookbook	Himalayan Institute
Meditation in Christianity	Himalayan Institute
Art and Science of Meditation	Himalayan Institute
Therapeutic Value of Yoga	Himalayan Institute
Chants from Eternity	Himalayan Institute
Spiritual Diary	Himalayan Institute
Blank Books	Himalayan Institute

Write for a free mail order catalog describing all our publications.